MUSEUM
CAREERS

A Practical Guide
for Students and Novices

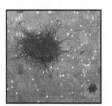

DEDICATED TO ALL THE Y'S AND S'S IN MY LIFE
AND ESPECIALLY LITTLE MISS M.

MUSEUM
CAREERS

A Practical Guide
for Students and Novices

N. Elizabeth Schlatter

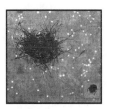

Routledge
Taylor & Francis Group

LONDON AND NEW YORK

First published 2008 by Left Coast Press, Inc.

Published 2016 by Routledge
2 Park Square, Milton Park, Abingdon, Oxon OX14 4RN
711 Third Avenue, New York, NY 10017, USA

Routledge is an imprint of the Taylor & Francis Group, an informa business

Library of Congress Cataloging-in-Publication Data

Schlatter, N. Elizabeth.
MUSEUM CAREERS
A practical guide for novices and students / N. Elizabeth Schlatter.
p. cm.
Includes bibliographical references and index.
ISBN 978-1-59874-043-1 (hardback : alk. paper) -- ISBN
978-1-59874-044-8 (pbk. : alk. paper)
1. Museums--Vocational guidance. 2. Museums--Employees. 3. Museum
techniques--Study and teaching (Higher) I. Title.
AM7.S27 2008
069.023--dc22
2008003812

Cover Image:
"Seraphim," 2005. by Tanja Softić.
Acrylic, charcoal, and chalk on handmade paper, 39 x 39 inches.
Copyright © 2005 Tanja Softić.

ISBN 978-1-59874-043-1 hardcover
ISBN 978-1-59874-044-8 paperback

CONTENTS

ACKNOWLEDGMENTS

Special thanks for guidance and assistance from Anthony Yanez, Doug and Dale Schlatter, Mark and Lynn Schlatter, Carolynne Harris, Marlene Rothacker, Sarah Clark-Langager, Annie Elliott, Sarah Falls, Donna Joyce, Joan Maitre, Tanja Softić, Michelle Torres Carmona, Richard Waller, Bradley Wright, the anonymous reviewers, and Mitch Allen.

THANKS ALSO TO THE FOLLOWING:

Dana Baldwin	Jackie Huffines
Shari Berman	Susan Jarvis
Barbara Blank	Lauren Telchin Katz
Lynda Brown	Olivia Kohler
Heather Campbell	Adam Lerner
Vernon S. Courtney	Eugene G. Maurakis
Noreen Cullen	Juanita Moore
Meg Eastman	Jackie Mullins
Ellen Efsic	Elizabeth S. G. Nicholson
Linda Eppich	Daniel Piersol
Heather Ferrell	Mike Rippy
Kerry Folan	Jennifer Pace Robinson
Tad Fruits	Terrie Rouse
Henley Guild	Scott Schweigert
David Hershey	Jeri Townley
D. D. Hilke	Neil deGrasse Tyson
Scott Hook	Richard Urban
Matthew Houle	Walter R. T. Witschey
Chuck Howarth	Antoinette Wright

And to all of the staff and faculty of the University of Richmond Museums, Boatwright Memorial Library, Modlin Center for the Arts, and Department of Art and Art History.

PART ONE
MUSEUM WORK

INTRODUCTION
WHY WORK IN A MUSEUM?

The museum where I work owns a print by American artist John Biggers (1924–2001) that I visit every time I enter our collections storage area. Titled "The Midnight Hour," the print is too sensitive to light damage to display permanently. Biggers gained widespread recognition for his accomplishments as an artist and teacher and was acclaimed for his depiction of African and African American themes. What pulls me into "The Midnight Hour," however, is not just the artist's trademark patterns, rich symbols, or rhythm of his abstracted forms, but a frankly narcissistic association I have with Biggers and my museum career. As an undergraduate gallery assistant, one of the first exhibitions I ever installed was a traveling show of Biggers's artwork. To this day, I recall hanging a particularly lush and entrancing painting and thinking, "This is what I want to do. This is it."

My early inklings of interest in museum work are typical of many in the profession, because working for a museum is both an altruistic yet selfish calling, dedicated to public education and enrichment. Typically, museums require hard work from an employee and offer relatively low or modest compensation. But museum workers have careers that feed their passions and expose them to new ideas, fascinating objects, and creative, stimulating environments. Even the crankiest museum staffers, who have been toiling away at a single institution their entire adult lives, will probably acknowledge they receive some sort of pleasure by working in a museum, such as passing an astounding dinosaur fossil or a beguiling Renaissance painting every time they walk to the accounting office or finding very hip and creative toys for their grandchildren in the museum gift store.

This interest in museum work, combined with a relatively small number of available positions, has resulted in a highly competitive environment for entry-, mid-, and senior-level jobs. A 2006 survey by the American Association of Museums (AAM) found that the median number of paid full-time staff at museums is six, and 6% of the respondent museums have no paid staff at all! Job seekers need a strategy to find openings and position themselves as strong candidates in the field of their choice, such as public relations, education, or curating.

There's no one direct route to a museum job. Although this may seem frustrating, it's actually very liberating, as people from all different backgrounds with a variety of skills and knowledge can become museum employees. The traditional trajectory still applies: Get an advanced degree, get an internship, get a job. But you'll find that some people discovered the museum world after gaining experience and skills acquired in other sectors, such as editing, gardening, teaching, and managing computer systems.

The goal of this book is to help you with that strategy from start to finish. You'll learn about different types of museum jobs, what kind of education and experience they require, where to find job listings, how to apply for jobs and conduct interviews, and how to begin your museum career. You'll read quotes from museum professionals who, unless otherwise noted, were interviewed for this publication and were eager to share their advice and experience.

You will not read declarative phrases such as "There are five critical positions in a museum. … " or "To get a job as a registrar you need to …" Instead, you'll find words and phrases like "may have," "probably are," and "most agree that," because there are many paths to becoming a museum professional. In fact, there's been a debate about whether museum work is a profession in itself or if museums are staffed by people working in various professions like accounting, public relations, publishing, etc. Regardless of the path you take, the rewards of museum work will be worth the effort.

REASONS PEOPLE WORK IN MUSEUMS
LOVE OF OBJECTS

If asked, many museum workers will probably cite a love of objects as a primary motivation for working in museums. Scott Schweigert, director of the Suzanne H. Arnold Art Gallery at Lebanon Valley College, Annville, Pennsylvania, chose the museum field over teaching art history full time because he was "seduced by the materiality of the objects. … I like keeping company with the results of an artist's creativity. So for me, being in a room filled with artwork held (and still holds) tremendous appeal; so much to look at, investigate, and learn."

Love of Museums

For some people in the field, their passion is quite simply the idea of museums—from the history of these special institutions to the psychology behind exhibition display to the multifaceted means to connect with the visitor. Many have received advanced degrees in museum studies or museum education; they read the magazine *Museum* cover to cover; and they regularly attend industry conferences to learn the latest developments in marketing strategies, fundraising campaigns, and exhibition display techniques. Having worked in museums for more than fifteen years, Carolynne Harris, a strategic planning consultant in Washington, DC, says:

> I love the fact that in working for museums, I am constantly exposed to new subject matter and enjoy thinking about the many choices that are made in presenting objects and ideas to an increasingly diverse public. I still find the big picture of museum work to be fascinating—to work on something that has the potential to truly inspire is a gift.

Positive Childhood Experience

A memorable childhood visit to a museum is commonly cited as an important influence in choosing to work in this field. Lauren Telchin Katz, planning specialist in the Office of the Director at the Smithsonian Institution's National Museum of American History (Washington, DC) recalls:

> My mother took me to The Metropolitan Museum of Art in New York when I was around 7 or 8 years old. I remember trying to touch the magnificent sphinx in the Egyptian art gallery to see if it was real. A security guard yelled at me not to touch it and I realized that this was a special kind of place. You could not touch things here—they were different and precious. This was an entirely new concept for my grabby fingers. I also remember that it was quiet—like a library—but much more exciting. People were busy looking at artifacts rather than reading or chatting. ... I started paying attention to what I was looking at instead of complaining that my feet hurt.

ENGAGING THE PUBLIC

The majority of museum professionals are motivated by the opportunity to engage the public, from a town's school system to the nation's top scholars. In its code of ethics for museums, the AAM succinctly defines the role of all museums as making a "unique contribution to the public by collecting, preserving, and interpreting the things of this world." Museums fulfill this function in myriad ways, such as at the Minnesota Historical Society in St. Paul, where the staff collects oral histories from the state's residents, at the Tallahassee Museum of History and Natural Science, Florida, which teaches children about the importance of understanding and preserving the natural environment, or at the Frick Collection in New York, where staff offer free lectures about eighteenth-century Baroque sculpture to museum visitors.

LIFE-LONG LEARNING

Because a museum is a center of informal learning for visitors, its employees can continuously explore their curiosity and passion for knowledge. Personally, I love art, and in my job I learn about art from different times and cultures to share its history and meaning with our visitors and its relevance to their lives today. As museum scientist and director of life sciences at the Science Museum of Virginia, Richmond, Eugene G. Maurakis enjoys

> the freedom to develop and conduct research projects in evolutionary and environmental science, using fishes as my organisms of choice. Additionally, the variety of research and programs that I am allowed to develop, fund, conduct, and publish, also are the basis of creating engaging, fun and challenging activities for visitors of the museum.

ENGAGING WORK ENVIRONMENTS

Because they attract creative and intelligent employees, museums encourage work environments that are innovative and invigorating—yet at times infuriating. Leading a dozen ingenious staff members can be a nightmare for a director trying to create a financially feasible strategic plan. Ellen Efsic, director of development at the Contemporary Arts Museum in Houston has noticed a recent shift in which, she says, more individuals with strong corporate backgrounds are taking leadership roles in nonprofits, and people with the arts background and passion are making an effort to study best practices in both corporate and nonprofit arenas. It works best where there's a combination of both.

THE DRAWBACKS OF MUSEUM WORK
MONEY, MONEY, MONEY

The opportunity to explore interests in art, education, history, and science and share this knowledge with the public motivates many people to make sacrifices to work in the museum industry. The primary sacrifice is money. For some people, museum salaries, especially starting rates, are simply too low to pay for basic needs, much less to be able to support a family. Because personnel costs are often the largest expense category for museums, salaries are often the first place museums look to minimize costs.

A quick overview of various salary surveys reveals that, not surprisingly, directors make the most money and retail clerks the least. (See Appendixes One and Two for examples from different salary surveys.) You can think of the totality of museum jobs in terms of a pyramid: at the bottom are the most jobs, which also have the lowest pay rates, from the $15,000s to the mid-$20,000s. These include entry-level positions such as assistants and service type jobs such as retail clerks, housekeeping, and security guards. The number of jobs shrinks as salaries rise, reaching the apex, which is an elite group of directors of very large, wealthy museums located in urban centers. They are paid in the six-figure range or more, including benefits and incentive packages.

Approximately twice a year, posters on the Museum-L listserve for museum professionals enter into a raging debate on why museum jobs pay so little and what can be done about it. Cited reasons include societal attitudes toward the "value" of museum work, the low salaries of all types of education-related jobs, the overuse of interns and volunteers, and the outdated idea that people working in museums are independently wealthy. Unfortunately, at this time, it's an employer's job market in the museum field. Museums can afford to offer low salaries because there are so many people eager to just get their foot in the door.

HOURS AND WORKLOAD

Museum employees often find themselves saddled with heavy workloads and mandatory overtime with after-hours programs or events. For staff who love their work, the days pass too quickly and they wish they had extra time to tackle their duties and accomplish their goals. As you move up the career ladder, even more time is demanded by the organization. For example, over the course of three days, a development director might work a full day, attend a private reception for major donors that evening, work another full day followed by an exhibition preview for members that night, present a new fundraising strategy at a breakfast meeting for board members the next day, all the while putting in additional hours preparing a grant application with an upcoming deadline.

GEOGRAPHIC LIMITATIONS

Another challenge for a person dedicated to a life in museums is the limited number of opportunities within their community, because of the limited number of museums in that community. For example, in a 2002 AAM survey, 71% of the responding science centers were based in large- or medium-size cities, 26% are in small cities or suburban towns, and only 3% hailed from small towns or rural/farm areas. A person dreaming of being a designer of the latest hi-tech science exhibitions will probably have to live in an urban center to find employment at an appropriate museum or design firm.

Even within cities, there may be few institutions in your chosen subject specialty. For example, if you want to devote your life to sharing your love of airplanes from World War II with others and you live in San Diego, chances are you'll want to work at the San Diego Air and Space Museum, but it may not have any job openings when you are seeking employment. Finding a comparable position in another museum might require relocating to another part of the country. However, if you are equally interested in teaching others about humanity's inventions and accomplishments, you might find a job as an educator at San Diego's Museum of Man, the Museum of Art, or the Hall of Champions Sports Museum.

Moving for any type of job can result in feeling like you are always in a steep learning curve, not just in the work environment but also in terms gaining a sense of a new city and forging new relationships. But

Ellen Efsic, who has worked at several institutions throughout her career, rightly notes that relocating "is often a faster track to promotion and compensation in the field." She says the main advantage to career growth attained by moving is being able to "gather a wide variety of experiences, learn lots of different nonprofit models, and make many contacts both professionally and personally."

There can also be perks to staying in one place. Until Hurricane Katrina struck in 2005, Daniel Piersol spent twenty-five years moving up the ladder through five different positions at the New Orleans Museum of Art to become the Doris Zemurray Stone Curator of Prints and Drawings. "If you're any good you build a reputation and gain the trust of the director, staff and trustees and you can really build up a great department and leave your stamp on it," he says. Some people refer to this as job equity that can only be developed by becoming a fixture of an institution and the local community. Ideally, your hard work and creativity will be recognized with promotions and raises. After the hurricane, Piersol's museum was forced to layoff the majority of the staff and he became the deputy director for programs at the Mississippi Museum of Art in Jackson.

But don't become too bogged down in the good versus the bad of museum work just yet. If you've picked up this book, chances are you have found something fascinating or exciting about museums already, and now you need to learn how you can turn your curiosity into a plan of action. The first step is to consider what types of museums may interest you and what opportunities they provide.

CHAPTER ONE

WHAT IS A MUSEUM?

As stated on its website, the International Council of Museums defines a museum as:

> A non-profit making, permanent institution in the service of society and of its development, and open to the public, which acquires, conserves, researches, communicates and exhibits, for purpoooo of study, education and enjoyment, material evidence of people and their environment.

AAM's code of ethics, provided on its website, states that the totality of museums includes:

> both governmental and private museums of anthropology, art, history, and natural history, aquariums, arboreta, art centers, botanical gardens, children's museums, historic sites, nature centers, planetariums, science and technology centers, and zoos.

There are myriad types of museums, and there is no national or international registry of these organizations. The AAM 2006 survey report estimates that roughly 17,500 museums operate in the United States. The annual *Official Museum Directory*—which in 2008 included more than 10,000 museums—is the largest published compendium of current U.S. museum listings, but submission is voluntary and not all museums are represented.

Moreover, there is no one standard museum organizational structure. A brief sampling of staff and job listings from museum websites quickly reveals this point. For example, the staff of the Amon Carter Museum in Fort Worth, Texas, includes a curator of paintings and sculpture and a distance learning coordinator; the Tryon Palace Historic Sites & Gardens in New Bern, North Carolina, employs a greenhouse manager and a domestic skills program manager; and the Monterey Bay

Aquarium in Monterey, California, has a curator of husbandry operations and a guest experience ambassador.

In general, museums can be categorized by four factors:

1. SIZE
2. GOVERNANCE STRUCTURE
   (the entity with legal authority for the museum)
3. GEOGRAPHIC LOCATION
4. DISCIPLINE (art, history, natural history, science, etc.)

These factors directly affect the job descriptions of people working within the same profession. For example, a director of a small private historical society in a tiny rural town might be the sole paid staff person, responsible for everything from planning exhibitions and programs to managing volunteers to fixing the plumbing. The director of a large, state-run natural history museum in an urban center might manage through delegation a staff of two hundred workers, oversee the development of a multi-million dollar expansion of the facility, and regularly report to the state government on how the institution serves the citizens.

SIZE

When people talk about the size of a museum, such as "I work at a small botanical garden," or "She runs a large art museum," they are referring mainly to its annual budget and number of staff, and not necessarily the physical size of the space. For example, a grand house museum with extensive grounds that employs less than five full-time people and operates on less than $300,000 per year could still be considered "small" in comparison to a contemporary art center with fifteen full-time staff members, a budget of $1.5 million, and only 4,000 square feet of exhibition space in a downtown warehouse.

Hundreds, if not thousands of museums have only one person on staff who may work part time or as an unpaid volunteer and who organizes the exhibitions, supervises volunteers and interns, runs all of the educational programs, and leads the fundraising efforts. As the number of staff increases, duties are delegated and jobs become more specialized. At a museum with a staff of five, the curator may also be the educator, so he or she researches the collection and organizes exhibitions as well as develops and implements all public programs, such as tours, lectures, teachers' workshops, etc. At a museum with twenty full-time employees, the curator of education may oversee a department of two, one being the person who develops and implements children's and school group programming and another staff member who oversees and trains volunteers and handles basic administrative duties. In addition to supervising this team, the curator of education creates and manages their budget, collaborates and coordinates with other departments, and develops adult programs such as seminars or film series. When staff numbers reach into the hundreds, the deputy director of education oversees several smaller divisions within his or her department, including visitor services, school and family programs, docents and volunteers, community outreach, and adult programs, for example.

The benefits and drawbacks of being employed at different sizes of museums reflect these levels of specialization. At a small museum, you not only observe but participate in almost all of the museum's operations, from facility maintenance to board communications. Your level of responsibility may grow rapidly as you prove your competence to the point of being in charge of your own projects. You will quickly learn what types of museum duties appeal to you, such as organizing members' receptions, and which ones do not, like writing grant applications. However, if the museum can only afford five employees, your opportunity for promotion is severely hampered and your salary may reflect the museum's limited budget.

Larger museums with well-staffed departments provide more opportunities for career growth—including increasingly sophisticated responsibilities and higher salaries—than smaller institutions. They also offer a greater number of professional contacts and the opportunity to specialize in your field, such as becoming a conservator of Islamic textiles or an educator focused on programs for inner-city elementary schools. Access to complex organizational policies and procedures can be enlightening and career enhancing when it provides you with the chance to create opportunities for yourself. Larger museums also convey prestige. Being a development assistant at the Field Museum in Chicago seems more impressive on your résumé than being a development assistant at a small-town arboretum, even though both jobs might have similar responsibilities.

The key to success at a large organization is working your way up the ladder, and that can be frustrating. Entry-level jobs at these institutions may be limited to very specific tasks that prevent creativity or intellectual activity, such as filing and data entry. At a small museum, you may find yourself spending three hours stuffing envelopes for a membership campaign, but you are also running the campaign yourself and can enjoy all the challenges and rewards of the project. Working in a highly specific job at a larger museum can also produce a myopic perspective on how the institution runs as a whole. For example, if you are the elementary school tour coordinator, you may never interact with anyone in the Conservation Department. But at a mid-sized museum, you might collaborate with a conservator to create programs that teach local collectors how to care for their own antiques or art collections.

When you are beginning your career, gaining experience at various sized museums allows you to acquire all of the benefits—a prestigious name on your résumé and a portfolio of accomplishments. You'll also gather a sense of which type of environment best suits your temperament and work style.

GOVERNANCE

The governing authority of a museum has legal and financial responsibility of the organization. That authority approves, rejects, and informs all of the museum's activities based on information gleaned from the staff's senior administrators and the museum's strategic plan.

Most **private nonprofit** museums are overseen by a board of trustees that ensures that the institution serves its mission and public. The term "private" means the museum is a nongovernmental organization and does not refer to the museum being open or not open to the public. These types of museums, like all private nonprofit organizations, are classified as "501(c)3"—a number that refers to the section in the U.S. Internal Revenue Code that exempts charitable organizations from having to pay federal income tax, unlike corporations. Nonprofits must apply to the IRS to receive this status, after which they can begin soliciting and accepting tax-deductible donations and become eligible for various federal and private granting opportunities, such as from foundations or individuals.

These museums raise their own income by means such as interest from an endowment fund (money that is invested), membership fees,

capital campaigns, admission fees, grants from foundations, corporations, or government agencies, fundraisers such as galas or auctions,
and retail sales or other auxiliary services like food service and cater-
ing. The variability of these income sources can result in job security
issues, particularly at smaller organizations that must constantly raise
funds for every aspect of their budget, from salaries and utilities to
exhibition costs and publications. Nonetheless, some independent
museums can be as large and stable as corporations; for example, The
Metropolitan Museum of Art in New York has more than 2,000 employees and an operating budget of over $180 million.

Museums that are not independently incorporated are often part of
parent organizations, such as universities, governments (national,
state, municipal, and county), tribes, foundations, corporations, or a
consortium of nonprofit entities. Examples of these kinds of museums
and their parent organizations include the Arizona Mining and Mineral
Museum, which is part of the state government of Arizona, and the
Memorial Art Gallery of the University of Rochester, New York, which is
part of the University of Rochester. Other kinds of parent organizations
include nonprofit associations that oversee multiple museums, often
historic sites such as the Nantucket Historical Association in
Massachusetts, which manages a Whaling Museum, an eighteenth-century Quaker meeting house, and the island's oldest house, which dates
to 1686. In a 2006 AAM survey, 35% of respondents said they were
overseen by a parent organization; roughly one-third of those are part
of a college or university.

Staff at these museums are usually considered employees of the
parent organization. For example, I work at the University of Richmond
Museums, so I am employed by the university itself, working in the
department of the museums. Being employed by the parent organization can convey job security and benefits not available at smaller
organizations, such as health insurance and retirement plans. Working
for the parent organization lures many people into the "system" who
never leave until retirement, making it difficult for others to find opportunities at the museum. However, lean years can result in cutbacks.
Following the devastation of Hurricane Katrina in 2005, the New
Orleans Museum of Art, which is a branch of the city government, was
forced to lay off seventy of its eighty-six employees.

Some very large corporations have created museums to document their history and influence, such as the Intel Museum in Santa Clara, California. The American Association for State and Local History (AASLH) developed a corporate history initiative to provide resources and networking opportunities for museum professionals working in corporate museums and archives.

A major drawback of working for a parent organization is the possibility that senior administrators cannot recognize the value of the museum to the community and are unable to discern a difference between running a museum and any other public department, like waste management. Layers of bureaucracy and administration can hamper or sometimes paralyze a museum's strategies or activities. And although the governmental authority contributes funds toward the museum's operations, the amount may fluctuate and be insufficient depending on politics and the economic climate, forcing the museum to raise funds for itself.

GEOGRAPHIC LOCATION

The following are just a few examples of how geographic location impacts the nature of a museum and its operations:

DISCIPLINE

This seems self-evident, but it's still worth mentioning that the location of many museums determines the subject matter of the collections, exhibitions, and public programs. The focus of the Alaska Historical Society in Anchorage is Alaska, and the focus of the Missouri History Museum is Missouri. Some museums focus primarily on their immediate physical location, such as the Molly Brown House Museum in Denver and the Arizona-Sonora Desert Museum in Tucson.

AUDIENCE AND COMMUNITY

As public educational institutions, museums serve their visitors and community and develop exhibitions and programs specifically for these audiences. Consider two museums, both in Manhattan: the Lower East Side Tenement Museum and The Metropolitan Museum of Art. Created with input from the community, the Tenement Museum occupies a former apartment building that housed immigrants for almost two centuries. Previous tenants and their family members became advisors to the museum's curators, teaching the staff about the history of the building and the people who lived there. The museum continues to collaborate with nearby residents and businesses to create special programs, such as walking tours of the neighborhood that examine historical and contemporary landmarks and issues.

Because it draws visitors from around the globe, the "community" of The Metropolitan Museum of Art in New York can be considered the world. Not only does the Met display art made from cultures from around the world, it offers on-site tours, maps, audio guides, and brochures in English, French, German, Italian, Japanese, Mandarin, and Spanish. Also, this multinational community can visit the Met because it is located in New York, a very large, international, and accessible city, as opposed to say, a small town in Idaho or even a mid-sized city like Milwaukee. At the same time, the Met offers a plethora of educational programs for local schools and organizations, thereby serving residents of its immediate geographic region.

FUNDING

Generally, the larger the city, the more money is available to support the arts and museums, hence the largest and most complex museums tend to exist in urban areas. The sheer amount and diversity of individuals, corporations, and foundations in cities provides a much larger donor pool than smaller, more rural regions. This axiom does not apply to state and municipal support. California is the most populated state in the country, yet its per capita spending on the arts is one of the lowest at just 3 cents per person annually in fiscal year 2006. The national average that year was $1.09 per capita, with Hawaii leading the ranking with $5.39 per person.

Also, some mid-size cities have industries, foundations, government agencies, or individual philanthropists who are highly engaged with and invest in the arts and museums. For example, Indianapolis boasts the Eiteljorg Museum of American Indians and Western Art, founded by local businessman Harrison Eiteljorg with funding assistance from the Lilly Endowment, Inc., a city-focused organization; the NCAA Hall of Champions, which opened when the sports organization moved to Indianapolis in 2000; and the Indiana State Museum, which has been part of the state's government since 1869.

DISCIPLINES

The following types of museums are described below:

1. ART MUSEUMS
2. HISTORY MUSEUMS
3. NATURAL HISTORY MUSEUMS/SCIENCE AND TECHNOLOGY CENTERS/PLANETARIUMS
4. OTHER: children's, zoos and aquariums, arboretums and botanical gardens, nature centers, general and specialized

ART MUSEUMS

Art museums collect, preserve, and display art, which, in general, includes statues, paintings, drawings, prints, photographs, decorative arts (e.g., Art Deco chairs or French Baroque punch bowls), and cultural artifacts (e.g., Egyptian sarcophagi or Mayan bowls). New technologies such as video or digital art can be found at museums with contemporary art exhibitions and collections.

An art museum with an "encyclopedic" collection owns the gamut of objects from around the world and created throughout history. For example, the collection of the Dallas Museum of Art in Texas ranges from ancient Greek vases to a seventeenth-century British dressing cabinet to a twentieth-century mask from the Kuba culture of the Democratic Republic of the Congo to a sculpture/installation made in 2002 by U.S. artist Matthew Barney. Encyclopedic can also characterize an extremely thorough collection of work that represents a certain culture, such as the collection of Chinese ceramics at the Asian Art Museum in San Francisco, which includes pieces from every time period and kiln throughout China from the past 4,500 years.

The German term *kunsthalle* refers to an art museum without any permanent collection. Instead, these museums, such as the Contemporary Arts Museum in Houston and the Wexner Center for the Arts at Ohio State University, Columbus, exhibit artwork borrowed from other museums, organizations, and people (artists or collectors), or they display new work created by an artist for that specific venue.

Different positions throughout the museum require varying levels of knowledge of art and art history, as the institution's mission infiltrates everyone's responsibilities. That is, if you want to work with objects at the Heard Museum in Phoenix, you'd better know a little something about American Indian art and culture when you show up for the interview. To curate, you'll need a doctorate or, at the very least, a master's degree in that field. Their conservators have been trained in working specifically with Native American objects and materials; their collections managers can probably cite NAGPRA (the Native American Graves Protection and Repatriation Act) word for word; the registrars know how to pack and handle sacred artifacts; the educators are versed in American Indian history and religion and the achievements of contemporary tribes; the public relations officer talks about the museum's activities to the general media (e.g., *The Arizona Republic* newspaper) as well as media targeted to Native Americans; and fundraisers write compelling grant applications about the museum's exhibitions and programs.

There is no one association specifically for art museum employees from all ranks. The Association of Art Museum Directors (AAMD) admits only elected members from institutions with annual budgets at or above $2 million. The Association of Art Museum Curators is open to anyone who holds a curatorial position at an AAMD member museum, although employees of non-AAMD museums can apply to join. Geared toward art and art history professors and students, the College Art Association does offer some resources for museum workers.

HISTORY MUSEUMS

There are more history museums than any other category in the United States. The 2001 edition of the *Directory of Historical Organizations in the United States and Canada* (AltaMira Press) included more than 12,000 institutions. In AAM's 2006 survey, 27.9% of the respondents identified themselves as history museums/historical societies, and another 10.1% said they were historic homes/sites.

History museums collect, maintain, study, and exhibit history, meaning the history of peoples, places, and/or things, including houses, parks, landmarks, and living history sites. They can be national or international in scope or locally focused. Their collections can include everything from physical objects and artifacts to oral histories.

The mission of the Smithsonian Institution's National Museum of American History is to inspire a broader understanding of the nation and its many peoples. Its collection includes more than three million artifacts, most famously the original Star-Spangled Banner, Abraham

Lincoln's top hat, and Dorothy's ruby slippers from the movie *The Wizard of Oz*. It has permanent exhibitions, which are always on view and feature objects in its collection, and temporary exhibitions, such as one that commemorated the events of September 11, 2001, through objects, images, and personal stories.

At **historic homes and sites**, the primary "object" preserved and maintained by the staff is the facility and/or grounds. These institutions must find a balance between allowing public access without jeopardizing the integrity of the site. In other words, a house built for a single family cannot withstand the trampling of hundreds of tourists per day. So, at many historic sites such as Frank Lloyd Wright's house Fallingwater in Pennsylvania, visitors can only enter the house itself if they take a timed guided tour, limited to a certain number of people.

When you visit a **living history museum**, you'll see people walking around in period costumes, giving tours, demonstrating crafts, and answering questions from visitors. These educators are called interpreters. Living history museums hire staff with varied backgrounds, such as a blacksmith who can demonstrate nineteenth-century techniques or a driver who will lead a horse and carriage full of visitors throughout the grounds.

As with all museum jobs, employees at these institutions should at the very least be enthusiastic if not knowledgeable about the museum's mission, collections, and programs. Directors and top-level curators at larger organizations possess doctorates, and several other mid- to high-level positions require some form of graduate degree, which could be in history, museums studies, conservation, museum education, or business administration. An undergraduate degree in history may suffice for smaller historical societies. Conservators might have experience working with a particular type of artifact, such as textiles or basketry or even architecture for a historic building museum. Registrars, collections managers, and preparators must be able to handle and properly care for myriad kinds of objects. For example, a preparator at the Atlanta History Center might move a nineteenth-century doll into the conservation lab, dress a dummy in a blue jean jacket and pants from the 1970s, and prop up an Appalachian fiddle in a display case. Education staff at history museums must be knowledgeable about their museum's focus, be able to create varied and engaging programs for visitors, and be good managers to oversee the many, sometimes hundreds of volunteers who give tours and interact with the public on a daily basis.

Staff at history museums have a plethora of organizations to join to find opportunities for professional development and networking. The largest, AASLH, is open to anyone interested and willing to pay dues. It publishes a quarterly magazine in addition to more than seventy books on issues affecting museums, and it offers national and regional workshops and seminars. There are also state and regional historical associations as well as organizations devoted to specific subjects such as the Association of Railway Museums and the Association for Living History, Farm, and Agricultural Museums.

NATURAL HISTORY MUSEUMS/
SCIENCE AND TECHNOLOGY CENTERS/PLANETARIUMS

Natural history museums focus on life and earth sciences, including ecology, geology, mineralogy, paleontology, zoology, and anthropology. Most natural history museums care for permanent collections in addition to organizing exhibitions and creating engaging programs. For example, the Field Museum in Chicago has a permanent display of "Sue," which is a large *Tyrannosaurus rex* fossil, an anthropological collection of more than 600,000 objects with a strong focus in East Asian artifacts, and a bird specimen collection numbering over 400,000. Collections in natural history museums often focus on regional animal and plant life as well as geology.

Science and technology centers differ from natural history museums by emphasizing exhibitions and hands-on displays that teach about concepts rather than focusing on collections objects or species. Founded in 1969, the Exploratorium in San Francisco is an industry leader in what it terms the "movement of the museum as education center." Instead of being faced with a life-size dinosaur or an eye-popping collection of gems and minerals, visitors to this museum encounter more than 600 interactive exhibits to touch, hear, see, and play with while learning about science. For example, one display called the Balancing Ball/Bernoulli Blower shows a large plastic beach ball "floating" above a plastic cone, out of which is blowing a strong stream of air. Visitors can pull the ball out of the air stream or rotate the cone to see how air can counteract gravity to support matter, which then facilitates understanding how airplanes fly. The

Exploratorium provides information about hundreds of such displays on its website for other museums that want to create their own versions or for educators to use in their classrooms.

If you've ever visited one, you'll know that a **planetarium** is a specially designed room or building that projects or simulates the sky—planets, stars, and other celestial bodies—onto a domed ceiling. Visitors sit in a theater-like arrangement and experience programs about astronomy, history, and science, in addition to the occasional Led Zeppelin laser light show and popular movies. Planetariums might be part of a natural history or science museum or can be stand-alone organizations, such as the Adler Planetarium and Astronomy Museum in Chicago, which celebrated its seventy-fifth anniversary in 2005.

Of course, there are overlaps in terms of what these museums offer their visitors. Many natural history museums now incorporate the theories and strategies of science centers, providing interactives and other opportunities for their onsite visitors to intellectually and physically engage with the study of natural sciences. And science centers may explore some topics similar to natural history museums, particularly animals, human health, and the environment.

Natural history museums, science and technology centers, and planetariums rely heavily on their education and exhibitions departments to make scientific research accessible to visitors and to foster an enthusiasm for learning. These staff members often outnumber curators and collections employees, particularly at science centers, and they typically have master's and undergraduate degrees in a science-related field, museum studies, design, or math or science education. Students from grades K–12 and families with children are the primary target audiences for these museums, so educators create a variety of programs and written materials to reach various ages and to meet state-defined educational curriculum. Exhibition developers at these types of institutions must balance the issue of presenting objects so that they can be examined without being damaged by the public or creating hands-on displays that will withstand the onslaught of thousands of school children with curious fingers.

Just as some staff working with objects at natural history museums are "jacks of all trades"—able to support and move a fungi sample or an enormous whale specimen—some are specialists, such as the collections manager for amphibians. Many museum curators have doctorates and research and publish in their field of interest while employed at the museum. So a curator might spend months in a cave in Central America studying bat habits, funded by the museum or an independent foundation. On returning to the museum, her or his research can be the basis of an article in a scholarly publication, used to better study and classify the museum's collection of bats, and form the basis of the upcoming blockbuster exhibition, "BATS!"

Major natural history and science museums have very large and sophisticated departments for marketing, fundraising, merchandising, public relations, and visitor services—making these types of museums particularly rewarding to staff with business backgrounds and a variety of nonscientifically oriented degrees and experience.

The Association of Science and Technology Centers (ASTC) offers a national conference, a bimonthly journal, and other professional development programs and resources for employees of all types of science museums. ASTC also has a searchable job bank. The Natural Science Collections Alliance serves any organization with a natural history collection, including museums, universities, and government agencies. Like ASTC, it offers an annual conference, publications, and job listings, in addition to other benefits. Both organizations work on behalf of science museums and institutions to define industry standards and to advocate their members' missions and roles in society. Organizations for planetarium employees include the International Planetarium Society and regional associations such as the Middle Atlantic Planetarium Society. The Association of Science Museum Directors promotes collaboration between institutions on research projects and programs while providing a forum for dialog and networking at their annual meetings.

OTHER DISCIPLINES

Although **children's museums** have existed since the Brooklyn Children's Museum was founded in 1899, the field exploded in the 1980s and 1990s, in large part because of the emphasis on the educational function of all types of museums. The Association of Children's Museums (ACM) defines children's museums as "institutions committed to serving the needs and interests of children by providing exhibits and programs that stimulate curiosity and motivate learning." These organizations provide children and their families a fun and safe environment for creative play and learning. Although the audience for children's museums is specific, the subjects of their exhibitions and programs vary greatly, with examples ranging from a walk-in model of the human digestive system to a children's garden to an exhibition about religious holidays from around the world. Mid- to upper-level staff at these museums usually have backgrounds and degrees in education, museum studies, or museum education. The ACM offers many opportunities for professional development, including guidelines on how to start a children's museum from the ground up.

Zoos and **aquariums** differ from natural history museums because they have live collections. To join the Association of Zoos and Aquariums (AZA), institutions must be accredited by the AZA, which means they meet or exceed industry standards, with the highest priority given to animal care and husbandry. So, in addition to general requirements such as a vigorous educational program that presents current information appropriate for the visitors, AZA members must adhere to facilities requirements and procedures governing the care of their collections. Examples include having enough indoor and outdoor space for each animal, exercising elephants daily, and following legal protocol for capturing animals in the wild.

In addition to jobs found at any type of museum such as public relations officer, retail manger, etc., zoos and aquariums have positions that require special skills, such as animal handlers and trainers, and jobs that require advanced degrees in biology, zoology, or veterinary science. The AZA offers courses for graduate credit as well as a master's in zoo and aquarium leadership through George Mason University in Virginia, which provides distance-learning options. Advanced education positions at these museums require graduate degrees in education or museum education, with knowledge of animal sciences.

Arboretums and botanical gardens are organizations dedicated to the appreciation and study of plants. They may be stand-alone institutions or be included in organizations such as zoos, art museums, nature centers, and historic homes, or they may be part of a university that uses the garden for research, as in the Arnold Arboretum of Harvard University. The American Public Gardens Association has more than 500 members throughout the country, even in states that might not come to mind when thinking of a traditional garden, such as the Alaska Botanical Garden in Anchorage and the Desert Botanical Garden in Phoenix. Top researchers in these organizations have doctorates in botany, ecology, or similar fields. In addition to fundraisers, public relations managers, and general administrators, public gardens might also have specialized jobs such as greenhouse manager, plant propagator, and grounds superintendent.

Nature centers straddle the line between zoos and botanical gardens, as they tend to feature large areas of land with native plants, birds, and wildlife in residence. Focused on caring for and educating the public about the environment, they might be located on a property that has been preserved from encroaching development. In addition to the zoo positions mentioned above (e.g., veterinarian, animal handler), nature centers hire botanists, groundskeepers, and many tour guides and educators.

Nine percent of the respondents in AAM's 2006 survey identified themselves as **general** museums, and just over 10% said they were **specialized**. General museums defy classification by combining several disciplines such as the Morris Museum in Morristown, New Jersey, which is dedicated to promoting the understanding and enjoyment of the visual and performing arts and the natural and physical sciences. Specialized museums focus on specific topics such as automobiles, aviation, railroading, maritime and agricultural history, religion, ethnicity, and sports. Many culturally or historically specific museums fall into this category, such as the Japanese American National Museum and the Southwest Museum of the American Indian, both in Los Angeles, and the U.S. Holocaust Memorial Museum in Washington, DC. Even more specialized examples include the Toy and Miniature Museum of Kansas City, the Museum of Jurassic Technology in Culver City, California, and the Rachel Carson Homestead in Springdale, Pennsylvania.

ONE FINAL NOTE

When applying for museum jobs that are not subject specific, you do not have to be intimately familiar with the discipline. But you should be knowledgeable about the museum's specialty and prepared to be enthusiastic about the institution's mission. A general rule of thumb for museum work is that if you dislike the mission, you'll hate your job. For example, a position as membership director at the Liberace Museum in Las Vegas can quickly become a curse if you aren't a piano music fan.

CHAPTER TWO
MUSEUM TRENDS AFFECTING EMPLOYMENT

At a thriving museum, visitors will experience something different each time they enter the building. For example, at a natural history museum, visitors may see a new display of fossils that reveals how ancient creatures used to thrive on the planet; view an award-winning film series on spiders; and hear their son or daughter explain the games and rituals of Mayan culture as explored in the pre-Columbian exhibition, thanks to the museum's outreach program in local public schools. A vibrant museum constantly strives to remain vital to the community at large, to offer the best care and maintenance of its collection, and to operate as efficiently as possible.

This chapter addresses major recent transformations in museums intended to improve their functions and operations. Because this book is focused on professional development and not museum studies, the trends have been chosen and are examined in relation to how they affect personnel. External forces initiating these changes include public demand, technological improvements, visitor demographics, competition with entertainment venues, and federal laws and regulations. Internal causes include budgetary needs, evolving responsibilities for specific jobs, and changing organizational hierarchies.

THE PRIMACY OF THE EDUCATOR
In his 1999 essay "From Being *about* Something to Being *for* Someone," museum scholar Stephen Weil discussed the sea change in American museums that took place during the 1980s and 1990s, when educating the visitor replaced object care as the primary mission of a museum. AAM's publication *Excellence and Equity* (1992) clarified this role and, in a sense, revivified these institutions by immersing them in the fabric of their communities through education. Education and exhibitions departments quickly sprang up and/or grew in size to meet these new demands. Exhibitions departments typically consist of people who

literally create exhibitions, meaning writers, designers, fabricators, interpreters, and project managers, as opposed to curators who traditionally study objects and write scholarly text. At small- and mid-sized museums, these responsibilities are often conflated.

Education and programs are blanket terms used for everything that impacts the museum's public—on-site, off-site, and virtual—including but not limited to lectures and performances, brochures, teachers' resource kits, tours, websites, workshops and demonstrations, and exhibitions. At the Art Institute of Chicago, education efforts run the gamut from "Cleopatra," which is an online resource for students to learn about the ancient world, to special programs for teachers to incorporate the museum in their curriculum, to illustrated lectures provided at senior centers, to the "Touch" gallery, where museum visitors are encouraged to handle selected artworks.

Even though this focus on education began about twenty years ago, the effects are still occurring, encouraged in part by changes in funding opportunities and by AAM initiatives. Foundations and government agencies offering support for museums tend to favor educational and community projects, as opposed to scholarly exhibitions and publications, collections care, or endowment campaigns. Museums seeking AAM accreditation must demonstrate how they learn about their visitors, use this knowledge to shape their programs with content and access appropriate to their communities, and evaluate the effectiveness of the museums' public activities. So, not only do educators create programs and exhibitions, they are tasked with collecting and analyzing data about program participants and their needs.

Degrees in museum education and exhibition development have professionalized these aspects of museum work. And any museum with outreach in its mission will strive to have a vibrant education department, often outnumbering staff in other departments, particularly at small- and mid-sized organizations. Although museum education and exhibition development offer many options for employment, staff in these departments are typically not paid any more than other employees, and grant-funded positions can be short term and nonrenewable.

THE SUBORDINATION OF THE CURATOR

In the past, curators were the "stars" of the museum world. They spent summers in Italy bargaining for ancient treasures, or being holed up in their offices writing volumes about a newly discovered beetle species, or canvassing small towns for WWII veterans to interview. They dreamt up fabulous exhibitions and gorgeous color catalogs, without worrying about how their activities would be financed or whether visitors would leave the museum any better educated or enriched than when they walked in the front doors.

But then came the rise of the educator, along with the accountant, the fundraiser, and the exhibition developer. Money usually spent on acquiring Ming dynasty bowls was now directed toward children's workshops. Instead of running meetings and deciding what objects to exhibit, the curator became a "team member." The development officer took the chair next to the director, and the curator was bumped further down the food chain Some museums, such as children's museums and science and technology centers, pride themselves on having no curators on staff at all.

As museum missions shifted from focusing on objects to focusing on visitors, they reorganized their staff structure and increased their education and exhibitions departments. The stereotypical curator of the mid-twentieth century (an overeducated male connoisseur who reveled in his acquisitions, arcane research, and elite insular network of peers) became obsolete. In an article in *Museum News*, Nancy Villa Bryck recalled her experience as a curator at the Henry Ford Museum and Greenfield Village in Michigan: "Until the 1990s, curators did not think that paying attention to the audience was our job. Now, we learned, it was everyone's job" (Bryck, p. 41). In fact, the Association of Art Museum Curators was founded directly out of this type of concern for the status and future of curators in the visual arts.

Today's curators work in tandem with fundraisers, educators, and exhibition developers by contributing their scholarship and creativity to exhibitions, programs, and publications. Some of their functions remain the same, such as researching and publishing about objects in a museum's collection. But at many museums, the education and exhibitions departments drive the museum's activities and organize exhibitions. The curators may or may not buttress these projects with research that is then "interpreted" to effectively communicate knowledge and ideas to visitors.

Even with their changing roles, curatorial jobs remain very competitive, despite low pay and equally low numbers of available positions, in part because of the intellectual and creative nature of the job that many people find appealing. Curatorial candidates are still required to possess advanced degrees: a master's in the museum's discipline at the very least, if not a doctorate. The strongest candidates demonstrate additional skills in terms of communications, fundraising, project management, and perhaps most importantly, being a team player.

TRANSPARENCY IN COLLECTIONS MANAGEMENT

With all of this focus on outreach and education and the importance of the visitor, one might think that collections management had faded into the background. But this basic function has become much more complicated since the 1990s, particularly in terms of repatriation and ethics violations, public access to collections, insurance policy changes, technology, and copyright issues. These fairly recent changes have created not only additional demands on the knowledge and skills of collections and registrarial staff, but in some cases new museum positions dedicated to these responsibilities.

At its simplest, proper collections management ensures that objects are securely stored and exhibited in a manner that does not adversely affect their condition. Temperature, humidity, and light levels are controlled carefully, and staff routinely check for pests or any changes in an object's condition, such as decomposition, mold growth, fading, or breakage. Similarly, registrars, conservators, and preparators are trained to properly handle myriad types of objects to minimize the occurrence of damage in transport and while on public display.

Museums also require collections staff to maintain meticulous documentation on the condition and history of the objects before and during the museum's possession. The history of an object is called its provenance, and it includes information on how the object entered the museum's collection (e.g., gift, purchase, or long-term loan), as well as previous owners and their transactions. For example, a painting made in 2005 and bought directly from the artist's dealer has a very simple provenance. But an ancient Greek vase given to a museum by a private collector might have a very long and even sketchy history of ownership, which at some point could have involved ill-gotten gains, such as looting or illegal exporting.

With such an object, confirming the rightful owner becomes an exceedingly complex matter. Several fairly recent initiatives have attempted to return art and artifacts currently held in museums to their originating owners, descendants, and/or cultures. For example, in 1990 the U.S. Congress passed the Native American Graves Protection and Repatriation Act (NAGPRA), which mandates federal agencies and federally funded institutions review their entire collections for any human remains and sacred or funerary objects of Native American origin, supply the National Park Service and registered tribal communities with inventories of these objects, and allow tribal representatives to visit and possibly reclaim the objects when appropriate.

AAM, the Association of Art Museum Directors (AAMD), and the International Council of Museums have created guidelines for museums to identify art and artifacts in their collections that were stolen from European citizens and institutions by the Nazis between 1933 and 1945 and never lawfully appropriated by the museum in possession. AAM's Nazi-Era Provenance Internet Portal serves as an online registry for museum reportage and for people searching to reclaim objects lost during the war. More recently, large encyclopedic museums, such as the J. Paul Getty Museum in Los Angeles and the Boston Museum of Fine Arts have been contacted by foreign governments—Italy, Greece, and Turkey, among others—requesting the return of cultural objects that were allegedly obtained illegally, either by the museum or their donors.

On the home front, AAM now requires an accredited museum to provide public access to its collections while maintaining proper care, as a means to becoming more transparent in terms of public trust and accountability. Because so few museums have enough space or manpower to exhibit every object in their possession, many have turned to technology to create searchable online databases or websites to offer intellectual access to their collections. For museums with ample room, another solution is open storage, in which many objects are grouped according to type and displayed together without didactic materials but in protected environments so that museum visitors can see thousands of items that normally would be available only to researchers.

Collectively, these developments have led to increasing numbers of collections managers, researchers, or even departments solely focused on provenance research and repatriation, collections digitization, or copyright research and protection. Meanwhile, the long-term effects of foreign governments requesting repatriation of art and artifacts from museums have yet to be determined.

ESCALATING USAGE AND
IMPACT OF INFORMATION TECHNOLOGY

Claiming technology as a trend in museums seems too obvious to mention. But museums must stay abreast of constantly changing technology, software, and means of digital communications to stay relevant to contemporary audiences.

In the 1980s and 1990s, museums began using computer hardware and software for as many functions as possible, such as databases for collections or donor records, retail and cafeteria operations, admissions, interactive exhibition kiosks, and audio/video devices. The Internet allowed museums to create websites, put resources such as teachers' kits or press releases online, sell their merchandise online, and organize virtual exhibitions based on objects in the collection or on display.

In 2002, the Institute of Museum and Library Services published a study that found 32% of surveyed museums were involved in digitization projects, with the primary goal of increasing access to the collections and records. This migration to virtual records has engendered jobs such as the visual resources manager who digitizes objects in the permanent collection and manages the database. It also increases the need for information technology (IT) and information services (IS) staff to support the servers, software, and content to ensure the stability and accessibility of the records. Often, these initiatives involve temporary grant-funded positions to conduct the legwork of the project, such as photographing objects, data entry, creating indexes, etc. At some point, a critical percentage of major collections will have been digitized and these projects will slow down or be replaced by some other trend involving accessibility to museum programs and collections.

Concerning outreach and public relations, some of the latest tools are podcasts, videocasts, and RSS feeds as well as using social networking sites, at least until the next wave of Internet development. All of which is to say that at mid- to large-size museums, skilled IT and IS staffers are always in demand.

Compared to other museum colleagues, salaries for information directors seem quite high, with a range of $65,000 to $85,000 and above being common at large institutions. And larger museums are where you'll find the bulk of these types of jobs, as smaller institutions usually cannot support the salaries and tech needs without grants and other dedicated sources of income. Many of these positions would pay more at other nonprofits, such as hospitals or universities, and considerably more in commercial businesses. So, museum IT and IS staff have to consider the benefits of their work environment and their amount of job satisfaction in lieu of higher pay, which is not an uncommon situation for many other museum jobs that translate out of the museum sector, such as graphic designer, editor, financial officer, and others.

INCREASING MARKETING ACTIVITIES

At a museum, marketing can encompass activities such as public relations, visitor services, branding, corporate fundraising, membership, and advertising—basically anything that helps the museum identify its market (visitors, members, shoppers, researchers, students, educators, and funders) and create strategies to reach and affect that market by determining and meeting their needs. In the past, some of these functions might have been considered an afterthought and not coordinated as one major effort. But over recent decades, museums have realized the benefits and necessity of a cohesive marketing strategy.

Why do museums need marketing anyway? In major metropolitan areas, museums that rely on foot traffic and sales for income compete with other entertainment or retail venues or other museums to attract warm bodies in their doors. Marketing campaigns are often built around special temporary exhibitions, luring visitors with the promise of a unique experience. An example would be a museum that organizes a blockbuster exhibition of Impressionist landscapes, pays for a major advertising campaign around the theme, initiates a membership drive to lure visitors to commit to the institution and save on admission, and develops or acquires new merchandise linked with the exhibition to increase retail sales.

Effective museum marketing complements the museum's overall mission by strengthening the organization's role in the community, attracting new and diverse audiences to the institution, and improving the museum's reputation and/or brand. At its best, this type of marketing upholds and furthers the museum's educational goals by bringing its "message" to the people who benefit from the organization's offerings.

Good marketing likewise can increase a museum's revenue, and that's when things become sticky because the motivation behind the marketing campaign and even the exhibitions and programs themselves can change from education to economics, and the needs of the visitors may be trumped by the promotion of the funders. Two examples that come to mind both involve the Guggenheim Museum in New York, which in 1998 organized an exhibition of motorcycles funded by BMW and in 2001 developed a show about clothes designer Giorgio Armani, who later, it was revealed, promised the museum a $15 million gift. Every time the museum promoted these shows, both companies received priceless advertising in addition to the prestige of being associated with the institution. These actions led some critics to call the museum "McGuggenheim," suggesting that anyone with enough money could buy the institution and exploit it for their own marketing needs. These two cases, in addition to other recent situations, have led AAMD and AAM to issue new standards of transparency when it comes to funders and their relationship with museums and their programs.

Smaller scale marketing-initiated activities at a museum might present entertainment events created to lure a particular segment of the community to the museum with hopes that they will return or even better, join as a member. Examples include "singles night" parties created to increase the institution's younger membership base. These types of programs can be troubling to those in the museum field who view them as purely social events and not educational. But others see them as essential for revitalizing once-stodgy institutions to appeal to current and future generations of supporters.

In other words, museum marketing is an expanding field that no doubt will continue for the foreseeable future. Strong job candidates will be those with business and marketing backgrounds. A combination of subject specialty knowledge also helps, such as double majoring in marketing and art history. Marketing positions in museums can be some of the better paying positions, but as with IT jobs, the marketing staff at museums might be tempted to leave the industry for the private sector for better salaries and benefits. And although some museums employ their own marketing staff, others contract with professional agencies to work on a single project or a portion thereof.

CHANGING RESPONSIBILITIES OF MUSEUM DIRECTORS

Today's museum director has a 24/7 job, with as many bosses as there are trustees, and a veritable money pit of an institution to run. Sure, elite directorships command six-figure salaries and enjoy loads of perks, but these careers rise or fall depending on fundraising prowess and fiscal management. That constant pressure, coupled with trying to manage the sometimes frustrating personalities of museum boards, volunteers, and staff, has resulted in an alarming rate of turnover for museum directors.

The contemporary director's workload may include leading a capital campaign for a building addition, overseeing an ambitious exhibition schedule that features blockbuster shows, and being the public face of the museum at press and fundraising events. At larger museums in particular, administrators look to business models for guidance in all areas of operations, from accounting to cafeteria sales to building construction to marketing. At some institutions, the increasing complexity of museum leadership has resulted in the creation of a top-level administrator to run all the business aspects of the museum, such as a chief financial officer or a vice president of administration and operations.

Until the late twentieth century, a museum was traditionally led by a scholar from a field represented by the museum's collection or mission, who had probably worked his way up from the curatorial ranks. But today's director might hail from a background in business, education, or fundraising. Boards hire directors from other nonprofits or the private sector with hopes that someone outside the system will bring a new skill set and a fresh approach to museum management. Not surprisingly, hiring outsiders often engenders frustration for insiders who have lost this opportunity for advancement and resent being led by someone unknowledgeable about the industry and its practices.

Walter Witschey, director of the Science Museum of Virginia says,

> The most interesting thing I notice about the directors of science centers is that, to a large degree, they did not come up through the ranks. There are exceptions, but I find that it is unusual for a number-two (such as chief operating officer) to become a museum CEO. They tend, instead, to have developed managerial skills elsewhere, and (fairly often) to have a strong science background. Boards tend to pick CEOs whose backgrounds provide the potential to deal with the museum's most urgent problem: financial crisis, old exhibitions, fundraising and endowment building, personnel management, marketing difficulties, or political challenges.

In her 2002 *Museum News* article on museum directors, scholar Majorie Schwarzer wrote that the typical museum director at that time was "a white 52-year-old with at least a master's degree. If J.Q. is female, she probably runs a small or medium-sized museum, rather than a large one." It is impossible to predict who the average museum director will be in ten or twenty years, but chances are the primary responsibility of directors in the future will remain fundraising, coupled with the increasing emphasis on accountability of funds and operations. And although new models of leadership may promote one quality over another, successful job candidates will continue to need superior communication skills to interact with all segments of the institution's public as well as the board, volunteers, and staff.

INCREASING STAFF DIVERSITY

Increasing staff diversity is not so much a trend but rather an industry-wide mandate that should become a priority and eventually an ingrained practice. Since the 1960s and 1970s, the museum industry has strived to become more inclusive in terms of engendering diverse audiences through educational programs and by adjusting the acquisition, maintenance, and exhibition of artifacts to better conform to their originating cultures' beliefs, rituals, and uses. Grants abound for museum outreach to underserved communities, such as inner-city school children, senior citizens in rural areas, and visitors with special needs. Examples of ways museums aim to reflect their own communities include incorporating signage in Spanish, creating advisory committees made up of local high school students who organize exhibitions and events themselves, and working with health associations to create tours for Alzheimer's patients.

But although museums' external functions have multiplied in variety, museum staff diversity remains stagnant at best. Few museum associations examine race, gender, sexual orientation, and disability in their statistical studies. In its 2003 report "A Business Case for Diversity," the Association of Zoos and Aquariums (AZA) found that less than 17% of accredited zoos and aquariums are led by women, and at a directors' retreat with about 150 participants, only one attendant represented a racial minority. The AZA compared its findings with that of the private sector to demonstrate how diversity is not just a moral imperative but also an important part of mirroring their community and targeting their "customers." It recommended creative recruiting to reach more qualified people in the workforce who may not know about opportunities in zoos and aquariums. Specific suggestions included advertising jobs on the Internet, participating in more job fairs, educating young children about these occupations, attracting diverse volunteers, and offering internships for workers of varying backgrounds.

As an African American museum professional, throughout his long and distinguished career Lonnie Bunch has often experienced being one of a handful of people of color at peer gatherings. Currently director of the Smithsonian Institution's National Museum of African and African American History and Culture, Bunch wrote in a 2000 article that although the field has diversified since the 1970s when he began attending national meetings of museum professionals, he is still disappointed by the limited minority presence in the ranks today. To reflect the diversity of the nation, diversity must become part of a museum's operations and identity:

> If museums are to be welcoming places for people of all racial, ethnic, social, economic, and education backgrounds, and if they are to use their collections to present a variety of perspectives, they must recruit, hire, or attract and foster the professional growth of trustees, staff, and volunteers who reflect diverse audiences and multiple perspectives. (Bunch, "Flies," p. 33)

Also overdue is an in-depth analysis of the gendering of the profession as a whole and within organizational structures, particularly looking at directorships and the seemingly overwhelming number of women staffing entry- to mid-level positions. Although some publications and articles from the 1980s and 1990s have focused on the topic of gender in museums, scant quantifiable information has been gathered; most is anecdotal.

Recently, the AAM developed guidelines for museums to create a diversity plan that would encompass everything from recruiting a diverse staff in all levels of leadership, to collaborating with local organizations, to fostering diverse audiences, to purchasing goods and services from businesses owned by women and minorities. And in 2004, the AAM approved a new Standing Professional Committee for Diversity in

Museums, charged to bring this issue to the forefront of the industry and to instigate change within the profession. The AAM also has related professional interest committees such as the Asian Pacific American Committee and the Alliance for Lesbian and Gay Concerns.

CONSULTING/OUTSOURCING

Finally, another important trend in museum employment is ... not working for a museum! You name the function, and I guarantee there is a freelancer or company out there that can be hired to perform it.

Museum **consultants** are people who have specific skill sets, expertise, and knowledge to perform sophisticated tasks to assist or advise the contracting organization. For example, a large museum considering undertaking a five-year capital campaign might hire a consultant to study the feasibility of such a project based on the economic climate and status of the museum in its community. Or perhaps a small museum was just given a grant to renovate an exhibition of Inuit artifacts. They might hire an education consultant to provide input on how to reorganize the display and provide information targeted to grade school teachers and students. In both cases, the consultants bring to the table specialized knowledge garnered after years of working in the industry and targeted to the museums' needs.

With **outsourcing**, museums hire a person or company to perform a specific service or task already defined by the museum. For example, some museums contract out their security or housekeeping staffs. Museums without conservation labs will pay outside professional conservators to work on art or artifacts, typically on a project-by-project basis. Other common outsourced functions include writing, editing, and designing large, complicated exhibitions or publications, curating in a subject area unfamiliar to the museum staff, marketing and public relations, crating and packing, shipping, and transporting objects and exhibitions. DC-based museum consultant Carolynne Harris notes that many museums have eliminated their internal exhibition design and fabrication departments. "This is the biggest, most established sector of outsourced services for museums right now," she says.

The two main reasons museums hire consultants or outsource work are to save money because they won't have to pay salary or benefits and to utilize someone's knowledge or experience that is beyond the capacity of the current museum staff. With specially funded projects such as the Inuit artifact example, it's much cheaper to hire a consultant to work on this finite project than for the museum to add a full- or even part-time staff member to the payroll. The consultant benefits by having control over her or his workload combined with flexibility. Harris says,

> As far as my own experience, I have absolutely loved it. For me, it has allowed for a good variety of projects and the luxury of not being caught up in internal politics of museums. Organizational issues and politics still have to be navigated, but I don't have to be engaged in them personally.

Often, these companies or consultants have cutting-edge methods and/or equipment to provide museums with new and effective approaches to various functions, especially in terms of technology. When museums reopen with new building expansions, overhauled displays of their permanent collection, and modern interactive exhibitions, they likely worked with outside architects, designers, and production companies to provide contemporary and engaging spaces and displays. Recognizing the potential profits, these companies now cater some of their services specifically to museums. Professional organizations are also welcoming museums into their community; at its annual expo, the International Association of Parks and Attractions offers more than a full day of sessions and presentations on topics relevant to museums.

Outsourcing and consulting can lead to chaos if the legal agreement between the museum and the contractor isn't thorough regarding every party's responsibilities and deadlines. AAM members can access guidelines, sample contracts, and Requests for Proposals through the organization's online information center. Harris notes that another struggle is finding clients.

> It is very stressful not to have a guaranteed salary income and it takes a certain amount of drive and discipline. As an independent consultant you spend half of your time marketing and doing administrative work, so that if you want to bill 40 hours a week, you work 80. And it's difficult to do marketing when you're really busy—another reason consulting can be somewhat cyclical (and stressful).

It's not uncommon for a consultant to be a former employee of the museum that has hired his or her services, although certain restrictions apply for consulting for governmental organizations. With a former employee acting as a consultant, the museum benefits by having someone already familiar with the institution working on the project. Likewise, the consultant may find him- or herself interested in or offered a full-time job with the museum, based on a successful project and working relationship.

If you are just beginning your museum career, you probably won't have the expertise to consult for museums but you may be able to work for a private company that provides services to museums. A job at an exhibition design and production firm will give you experience in these functions in addition to contacts that you can use later in your career. Some of the larger consulting firms might have entry-level administrative positions that can also provide entrée into the museum business. You can find some of these firms through AAM's online marketplace of vendors.

PART TWO
MUSEUM JOBS

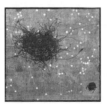

MUSEUM JOBS

This portion of the book focuses on positions that are fairly common in museums throughout the United States. Because each museum is different and the industry is constantly evolving, a grand compendium of every single museum job doesn't exist. For highly specialized jobs (such as antique lace restorer), try searching the web for professional associations relevant to the position (in this case, I'd try the American Institute for Conservation).

The jobs are grouped as follows:

CHAPTER THREE
JOBS FOCUSED ON OBJECTS AND/OR EXHIBITIONS

- **CONSERVATOR**
- **CURATOR**
- **DESIGNER**
- **EXHIBITION MANAGER/DEVELOPER**
- **LIBRARIAN/ARCHIVIST**
- **PHOTOGRAPHER**
- **PREPARATOR/ART HANDLER**
- **REGISTRAR/COLLECTIONS MANAGER**

CHAPTER FOUR
JOBS WITH A PUBLIC FOCUS

- **DEVELOPMENT OFFICER/MEMBERSHIP MANAGER**
- **EDITOR**
- **EDUCATOR/VOLUNTEER MANAGER**
- **INFORMATION OFFICER**
- **MARKETING MANAGER/PUBLIC RELATIONS MANAGER**
- **RETAIL MANAGER**
- **SECURITY CHIEF**
- **VISITOR SERVICES MANAGER**

CHAPTER FIVE
JOBS WITH AN ADMINISTRATIVE FOCUS

- ADMINISTRATOR/FINANCE OFFICER
- FACILITIES MANAGER
- GENERAL COUNSEL/ATTORNEY
- HUMAN RESOURCES MANAGER
- TECHNOLOGY OFFICER

CHAPTER SIX
THE DIRECTOR

Some jobs could easily shift from one category to another, especially considering that many of their responsibilities ultimately focus on the visiting public. But the groupings demonstrate how these positions relate to each other within the institution and are intended to provide you with several options to consider when searching for jobs. At smaller museums, many of the functions of these different jobs are combined. For example, a museum of only three full-time staff might have:

> • a director who handles all the administrative functions, facility needs, and the fundraising, so she acts as director, development officer, membership manager, administrator, human resources officer, and facility manager;

> • a curator who develops all the exhibitions and cares for all of the objects in the collection. He acts as the curator, exhibitions developer, collections manager, registrar, preparator, archivist, librarian, and conservator; and

> • an educator who creates all the educational planning, oversees all the volunteers who also act as security, handles all of the press and advertising, and knows how to fix computers. She's the educator, public relations and marketing manager, volunteer and visitor services manager, and the IT person.

As museum staffs increase in number, fewer responsibilities are combined. So a museum with eight workers might have a collections manager/registrar, a public relations/marketing manager, and so on, in addition to assistants who help with the workload (e.g., an assistant registrar or a public relations assistant). As museums increase in size, people specialize within their field as departments become larger and larger, allowing for positions such as traveling exhibitions registrar, director of major gifts, or coordinator for school tours. And some positions are only found at larger museums with resources and complex organizational structures that require and can support jobs like human resources manager, retail services director, and digital archivist.

Each position entry in this book includes basic descriptions, typical career ladders and salary information, requirements for education and experience, and sources for job listings and professional development. Because job listings posted by the American Association of Museums are comprehensive to the museum community, that organization won't be mentioned as a specific source. But always check its online job bank for opportunities, as well as some of the other regional and national organizations listed in Appendix Three.

Jobs that Are Not Included

Although many of the positions in this book apply to zoos, aquariums, gardens, and any other type of institution with live collections, I have not included jobs specific to these types of museums that require advance degrees in the sciences or highly specialized work experience, such as animal husbandry or plant propagation. For more information on these jobs, as well as educational and internship opportunities, see the websites for the Association of Zoos and Aquariums and the American Public Gardens Association.

A Note about Salary Ranges

The salary ranges and career ladders provided in this book should be used as guidelines only and are not to be construed as mathematical averages for the profession as a whole. They are based on my observations from published and unpublished salary surveys, job listings, and job descriptions. Salaries for similar positions vary greatly depending on the size of the institution, its mission, and its geographic location.

A NOTE ABOUT TRUSTEES AND VOLUNTEERS

Before going any further, I want to issue words of praise to board members and volunteers. These people freely contribute countless crucial hours and sometimes money to the leadership and operations of museums.

A museum **board of trustees** is a group of people legally responsible for the museum as a public trust. Typically, they are appointed to the board through nomination and election and serve predetermined terms, such as two to three years, that may be renewable. These trustees hire the museum director, who then implements the board's strategies as well as reports back on the museum's progress and operations. A prime responsibility of board members is to financially assist the museum, either through direct contribution or fundraising activities.

The relationship between trustees and the director is a delicate partnership and can be strained, particularly when power struggles occur. For more information on boards, see Boardsource, an organization dedicated to assisting directors and board members of nonprofits. There's no better way to learn about how boards operate than to join one, whether it's the board at the local historical society, the nearby animal shelter, or a mentoring organization for at-risk children.

Volunteers are those amazing people who offer their time and expertise to the museum free of charge to assist with specific tasks. At many museums, volunteers are the public face of the institution. They greet you at the front desk, offer to sell you a membership, give you a tour of the exhibition, and might even ring up your sales in the gift store. A **docent** is a volunteer tour guide who has undergone extensive training to speak about exhibitions or items in the museum's collection to different segments of the museum's audience, such as schoolchildren, the general public, or older adults. Because visitors might not be able to distinguish between volunteers and staff, volunteers are carefully trained to provide accurate information and assist museum goers.

Behind-the-scenes volunteers might be tucked away in the collections storage area, helping catalog and identify artifacts. Once, when I toured the basement of the San Diego Air and Space Museum, I met several retired military pilots who spent part of their days sorting, caring for, and researching everything from airline promotional posters to aircraft parts dating to the nineteenth century.

Volunteers also assist with organizing fundraising events such as galas or benefit auctions. They buy and sell tickets, help market the event to friends and companies, determine the event theme and location, work with contractors (such as florists and musicians), and may even decorate the venue themselves.

Museums benefit from volunteers in several ways. Volunteers provide services that the museum may not be able to afford, so the museum is subsequently able to offer more services for free to visitors, such as additional tours or educational programs. Loyal volunteers promote the museum informally to their friends and colleagues, helping to spread the mission to additional communities.

Volunteers benefit by the enjoyment of helping others and being part of an important organization. They often find themselves in intellectually challenging environments that call for their experience and expertise. They meet people with similar interests and talents and are surrounded by fascinating art, objects, or specimens. In some communities, being a museum volunteer, particularly a docent, lends a certain prestige, and these unpaid positions can be quite competitive.

CHAPTER THREE

JOBS FOCUSED ON OBJECTS AND/OR EXHIBITIONS

Jobs in this chapter involve working with objects and/or exhibitions, although they all have an additional focus on visitors and education, especially designers and exhibition managers. They are grouped together because people working in these jobs share essential skills and knowledge. With their related responsibilities, people in these positions often work together on complex projects, such as creating exhibitions and organizing and caring for permanent collections. Jobs discussed in this chapter are

- **CONSERVATOR**
- **CURATOR**
- **DESIGNER**
- **EXHIBITION MANAGER/DEVELOPER**
- **LIBRARIAN/ARCHIVIST**
- **PHOTOGRAPHER**
- **PREPARATOR/ART HANDLER**
- **REGISTRAR/COLLECTIONS MANAGER**

CONSERVATOR

The museum conservator protects, repairs, restores, cleans, and preserves objects in the museum's collection. The conservator works closely with collections managers, registrars, and curators to assist with the storage, handling, and study of artifacts. Conservators possess a combination of scientific knowledge and a level of skill and dexterity gained through experience working with actual objects, often acquired through apprenticeships. They typically specialize in various media, such as architecture, books, furniture, metals, paintings, photographs, textiles, works on paper (letters or drawings), and even objects from specific cultures, such as American Indian artifacts. And they use increasingly sophisticated software and equipment to image, analyze, and treat objects.

Museum conservators follow the "Code of Ethics and Guidelines for Practice," established by the American Institute for Conservation of Historic & Artistic Works (AIC). Similar to the medical practice, an important principle of that code is "First do no harm," by which conservators "must strive to select methods and materials that, to the best of current knowledge, do not adversely affect cultural property or its future examination, scientific investigation, treatment, or function." Or as one conservator once told me, "Whatever we do to a painting must be able to be undone easily by someone in the future."

Within the competitive world of museum jobs, conservator might just be the most challenging to break into because of the required levels of education and experience and the paucity of jobs outside of the largest institutions. Meg Eastman, conservation assistant at the Virginia Museum of Fine Arts, Richmond, says that the few schools with programs in conservation typically accept only ten or so students per year. She says,

> They look for "pre-program" experience which is hard to come by because no one really wants you in a conservation studio until you have some training under your belt. School is a three-year program; the third year is an internship with a museum or a private practitioner. Typically, the five years following graduation are spent doing fellowships (if you can get them—they're even more competitive than getting into school).

The costs associated with hiring a full-time staff and setting up and maintaining a lab limit the number of conservator positions overall. Most conservators work at mid- to large-sized museums with extensive collections and funding. Smaller institutions often contract out their conservation needs to freelance conservators or conservation firms. An independent conservator in a town with many museums that have no in-house staff can forge a successful business for him or herself, also garnering work from auction houses, dealers, and individual and corporate collectors.

CAREER LADDER AND SALARY RANGES
CONSERVATION ASSISTANT: $25,000 to $40,000

ASSISTANT CONSERVATOR: $30,000 to $50,000
CONSERVATOR: $45,000 to $70,000
CHIEF CONSERVATOR: $55,000 to $90,000+
   (over $100,000 for the largest museums)

EDUCATION AND EXPERIENCE

An undergraduate degree in studio art and/or chemistry and an advanced degree in conservation are required for all positions above the assistant level. Some of the preeminent graduate programs in conservation include Buffalo State University of New York, New York University, the UCLA/Getty Program in Archeological and Ethnographic Conservation, the University of Texas, Austin, and the University of Delaware. The latter two offer doctorates in preservation studies. Years of experience under trained conservators working with the chosen medium is required and often provided through these degree programs.

JOB ANNOUNCEMENTS AND PROFESSIONAL DEVELOPMENT

Look for job openings and educational opportunities on the AIC's website. It even offers online courses to help establish yourself as an independent conservator. Additional organizations include Heritage Preservation, the National Center for Preservation Technology and Training—which is part of the National Park Service—the Getty Conservation Institute, and the Campbell Center for Historic Preservation in Mount Carroll, Illinois. The website Conservation OnLine offers countless resources for conservator training, standards, and networking.

CURATOR

Traditionally, a curator is in charge of the museum's collections and exhibitions and has the following main responsibilities:

- study and interpret a museum's permanent collection and recommend objects for its growth and focus;

- organize exhibitions, including developing the themes, choosing objects, writing text, and overseeing the installation; and

- publish articles, catalogs, and books about the museum's collections, its exhibitions, and the curator's own field of research.

Since the emergence of education as the primary mission of museums in the 1970s and 1980s, responsibility #2 has moved out of the realm of curators into that of education and exhibition departments, often based on directives from the museum's top administrators. Rest assured, there are still hundreds if not thousands of museums in the United States where the curator is still in charge of creating exhibitions, and at the smallest institutions, she or he is the one literally hanging the work on the walls and vacuuming the carpets before the openings. But at natural history, science, history, and children's museums, the exhibitions and/or education departments often manage all if not most of the development, installation, and evaluation of exhibitions.

To overgeneralize, art and history curators spend the majority of their time focused primarily on their museums' collections, exhibitions, and publications, whereas science and natural history curators can spend a fair amount of their time performing research off-site and publishing within their academic field. The former group works closely with other museum professionals focused on object care and display as well as education, exhibitions, and often fundraising. In fact, the more experience curators have with fundraising, particularly in terms of grant writing and donor cultivation, the better they may realize their exhibition and collections goals (as in life, so in museums—money talks!).

Science and natural history curators often have positions akin to that of professors; in fact, many teach at universities and work in museums simultaneously, which supports the extensive fieldwork necessary for research and publication. For example, a curator of amphibians could spend months in a South American rainforest researching a vanishing frog species and gathering information that will be published later in related scholarly journals. On exhibition project teams, this curator will act as a consultant, providing the scholarly groundwork for the show but not actually writing the text or interpreting the materials for the visitor. Those tasks will be conducted by exhibition developers and educators.

At large museums, curatorial departments may be divided by mediums such as staff who concentrate on paintings, textiles, furniture, works on paper, etc.; sciences such as archeology, paleontology, or geology; or cultures and time periods like early American Indian cultures, nineteenth-century political history, or Midwestern agricultural history. At smaller museums, the curator usually reports to the director. At bigger institutions, one person may be in charge of all object and exhibition-related activities, with a title such as director of museum services or head of collections and exhibitions, who then reports to the museum's CEO.

CAREER LADDER AND SALARY RANGES
CURATORIAL ASSISTANT: $21,000 to $35,000
ASSISTANT/ASSOCIATE CURATOR: $25,000 to $40,000
CURATOR: $35,000 to $60,000
CHIEF CURATOR: $43,000 to $70,000+
(over $100,000 for the largest museums)

EDUCATION AND EXPERIENCE
At the very least, curators must have an undergraduate degree in the subject area of the museum, if not a master's or doctorate, particularly for senior-level positions. A master's degree in museum studies or curatorial studies may be applicable, especially if combined with work experience involving studying and writing about objects within an institutional setting.

JOB ANNOUNCEMENTS AND PROFESSIONAL DEVELOPMENT
There's no one source for listings of curatorial jobs, so besides checking AAM's listings, see those posted by organizations devoted to specific disciplines, such as the Association of Art Museum Curators, the American Association for State and Local History, and the Association of Science and Technology Centers. Positions within universities are often posted on the website for *The Chronicle of Higher Education* as well as higheredjobs.com and sciencejobs.com.

DESIGNER
Using software such as Vectorworks, AutoCAD, InDesign, Illustrator, and Photoshop, museum designers transform the content provided by various departments into engaging and accessible forms, either in 2-D

with printed or online material or in 3-D with exhibitions and products. The designers collaborate with educators to best present information and graphics and evaluate their effectiveness and with the Facilities Department to produce structures and visitor traffic patterns that are safe and conducive to the museum, which is called wayfinding. They might also help create retail products and printed materials such as advertisements, brochures, and gift items as part of an exhibition's promotion or the museum's brand identity. Museums with extensive online content and activities hire dedicated web designers who work within the Information Systems Department.

Throughout the exhibition development process, the designer will produce and present to the project team drawings, renderings, physical models, computer models, or mechanical prototypes for consideration and feedback before determining the final designs, which will be fabricated in-house or by outside firms. Much of this work involves strong communication and collaborative skills to best interpret into a graphic format the goals of the exhibition team, which, in addition to curators, educators, and exhibition staff members, may include registrars, conservators, information technology and systems staff, and marketing and visitor services workers. The designer may also handle bids and contracts and act as a project manager for outside design and production work. Designers report to the head of communications and marketing or the exhibition manager, especially if their responsibilities are more closely tied to exhibition design than to other products.

Shari Berman is a partner at the Brooklyn-based firm of Evidence Design, which offers exhibition, graphic, architecture, and interior design, as well as general museum and interpretive planning to their clients. "In short," Berman says:

> What I love about exhibit design is both the interdisciplinary and collaborative nature of the projects and the endless varieties of subjects that may be explored. Since USHMM [the U.S. Holocaust Memorial Museum, a past client], I have worked with paleontologists, geologists, anthropologists, historians, biologists, ornithologists, and evolutionary scientists. At Evidence Design, we are engaged with nuclear physicists, chemical engineers, mechanical engineers, meteorologists, aerospace engineers, material scientists, media

artists, sculptors, animators—the list goes on. It is a design profession that allows one to practice design, while constantly learning about the world around you—like being a perpetual university student.

Because both web and exhibition design require specialized experience and skills, particularly at natural history, science, and children's museums, museums often outsource these responsibilities. So, when seeking to enter this profession, people should consider positions at design and production firms that service the museum industry. Berman says:

> It is an expensive endeavor for museums to be able to sustain an internal staff of architects, industrial designers, media designers, project managers and the associated equipment required to execute exhibits on this level unless they have deep pockets and are constantly mounting new exhibits—let alone keep up with rapidly developing new technology, materials, and techniques.

Career Ladder and Salary Ranges
Design Assistant: $25,000 to $40,000
Graphic Designer: $35,000 to $50,000
Exhibition Designer: $40,000 to $65,000
Chief Exhibition Designer/Chief of Design: $50,000 to $75,000+

Education and Experience
An undergraduate degree in graphic design, architecture, interior design, industrial design, or theater design is required; graduate degrees in the same are preferred. The Fashion Institute of Technology in New York and The University of the Arts in Philadelphia are two of the very few schools offering degrees in exhibition design (associates degree and M.F.A. respectively). Job candidates must have experience with design software that is standard for the industry and should be able to present interviewers with a digital or hard copy portfolio of images from previous projects.

AAM's National Association for Museum Exhibition offers some job listings and professional development opportunities. Also see the general design employment websites such as coroflot.com and creativehotlist.com. The Society for Environmental Graphic Design and the Industrial Designers Society of America also offer job listings and professional development.

EXHIBITION MANAGER/DEVELOPER

Managing a museum's exhibition program can entail varying responsibilities, including developing exhibitions, selecting and overseeing incoming and outgoing traveling exhibitions, exhibition design, fabrication, installation, maintenance, and deinstallation. As the team leaders for these projects, exhibition managers work with the curator or content specialist, educators, and other exhibitions staff members, providing the vision to create exhibitions based on sound scholarship that will engage the museum's audience and attract new visitors. They assist in generating exhibition topics, interpret content based on research, collaborate with designers and fabricators to produce exhibitions that effectively convey the content to visitors, and evaluate exhibition components and usage to determine if the exhibition goals have been attained and are balanced in terms of educational mission, audience development, and marketing targets.

Prior to being vice president for experience development/family learning at the Children's Museum of Indianapolis, Jennifer Pace Robinson was their director of exhibit development. The job of developing exhibitions was especially appealing to Pace Robinson.

> You get the chance to be creative, generate ideas, do research, write concepts and then work with other talents to implement plans. It is a great combination of creative yet detailed work. When I was an undergrad, I was very unsure what to do next—I wasn't going to law school, med school, or even business or sales. I didn't know what I could do with my creativity and writing skills. Exhibit development is a "hidden" career that is hard to discover unless you get into a museum through an internship.

Part of the exhibition managers' job is akin to that of a project manager in other nonprofit or commercial sectors. They develop budgets and schedules of completion for their projects and monitor their progress to prevent cost overruns and missed deadlines. They ensure that the many people on the project team communicate effectively and oversee any outside contractors working on exhibitions. Chances are, they have dozens of projects in progress concurrently that they juggle at any one time.

They constantly educate themselves on trends and developments in exhibition design, fabrication, interactive technology, visitor behavior, educational models, and exhibition assessment to ensure that their exhibitions communicate the primary themes of the show, protect any objects, artifacts or specimens on display, and encourage visitor interaction in a safe environment. They also assist in canvassing opportunities for projects with curators, educators, and marketing staff and take leading roles in any sort of capital expansion projects involving exhibitions and visitors.

The exhibitions departments at large museums may include specialists such as graphic designers or exhibition scriptwriters, but they also may contract out design and production of particularly complex exhibitions, entirely or in part. Large museums hire one or more exhibitions managers who focus solely on administering and promoting traveling exhibitions. They oversee all the logistical needs of a touring show, including packing and crating, shipping, securing venues for the tour, and issuing contracts with museums hosting the exhibition.

In general, art museums tend to have the smallest number of dedicated exhibitions staff only because the other types of museums tend to have more complicated exhibition design, fabrication, and installation needs. In fact, some science centers and children's museums have no curators on staff at all. Instead, their large exhibitions and education departments develop all of their exhibitions and permanent displays.

Regarding the exhibition manager's place within a typical museum hierarchy, Pace Robinson says:

> The structure is probably very different in different types of museums. In most instances in natural history, science centers, and children's museums, there is a separate Exhibit Department. Most large art museums also have an Exhibit Department,

although exhibit matters are strongly directed by curatorial staff. Throughout various periods of my work, I have supervised exhibit developers, project managers, exhibit managers and audio/video staff. Our situation is a little different because we also have a director of production and design who supervises exhibit fabricators and designers. In most instances, I believe the director of exhibits would supervise all of these staff together.

CAREER LADDER AND SALARY RANGES
EXHIBITIONS ASSISTANT: $20,000 to $35,000
ASSISTANT/ASSOCIATE EXHIBITIONS MANAGER/COORDINATOR: $30,000 to $50,000
HEAD OF EXHIBITIONS/DIRECTOR OF EXHIBITIONS: $48,000 to $75,000+ (more than $100,000 for head of public programs/dimension at largest institutions)

EDUCATION, EXPERIENCE, AND SKILLS

An undergraduate degree in design, business, communication, education, or subject area of the museum is required. Advanced degrees in education, museum studies, the museum's discipline, or arts administration are desirable. The University of the Arts in Philadelphia is one of the few universities to offer a master's degree in Museum Exhibition Planning and Design.

Preferred experience includes any positions involving working with museum education, design, and project management. Some entry-level or technician positions may require experience with tools, processes, and software to physically produce and/or design exhibition components. Pace Robinson advises anyone interested in the career to start with positions involving museum visitors:

> This could be teaching workshops or working with interpretive programs on the gallery floor. The best exhibit developers have actually worked on the floor with children and families. They understand how people think and learn and can translate complex topics to the general public.

JOB ANNOUNCEMENTS AND PROFESSIONAL DEVELOPMENT

Besides AAM, for job listings and professional development see the

National Association for Museum Exhibition, which, among other things publishes a journal titled *Exhibitionist*. Also see job banks on websites for discipline specific museums, such as the Association of Zoos and Aquariums or the Association of Science and Technology Centers. And look at the "Museum Marketplace" on AAM's website, which has links to companies and consultants that provide exhibition management and development services.

LIBRARIAN/ARCHIVIST

The responsibilities of a contemporary librarian and archivist encompass a range of tasks focused on providing access to information and the preservation of the sources of that information. The two professions are closely linked because of the similarity in types of materials they work with, such as paper and digital records, and in the tools they use, especially cataloging software and standards.

Museum libraries contain myriad sources of information, including published materials such as books and magazines as well as mixed and sometimes aging media such as movies on DVDs, microfilms of newspapers, or oral history recordings on analog tapes. Museum libraries differ from public or academic libraries because they tend to be focused on object-oriented research rather than encyclopedic study. This means they may have fewer books on Impressionism in general than a university library but they will have as many publications and printed materials like articles, exhibition brochures, etc., possible relating to the Monet watercolor of haystacks that is hanging in the museum's wing of French art. The library might also have an extensive collection of publications on informal education and visitor research as it relates to the organization's mission, particularly at education-oriented museums like science and technology centers and children's museums.

The Society of American Archivists (SAA) defines archives as "noncurrent records of individuals, groups, institutions, and governments that contain information of enduring value." A museum's archives could include materials relating to their discipline and collection such as a diary written by a scientist on an expedition in Antarctica or to the museum's own history (e.g., organizational by-laws, board meeting notes, and photographs of the facility through various renovations). Linda Eppich, conservation projects coordinator/archivist at the

Preservation Society of Newport County, Rhode Island, says:

> There is a growing interest in museums to gather their own
> institutional information for posterity. That is how my job
> came about ... the interest in the PSNC 60th anniversary in
> 2005. I handle board and other committee minutes, process-
> es of getting things done, previous publications, and even
> the Society's AAM accreditation records—all 15 notebooks of
> it! And then there's the occasional original document and all
> those wonderful photographs!

Museum libraries and archives may have very limited on-site public
access, which is intended to protect the library's holdings and to ensure
that the museum's staff has priority usage. As caretakers for their collections, librarians and archivists learn about proper handling, storage,
and minor restoration of their materials and sometimes assist in the
preparation of exhibits featuring items in their collections.

To fulfill their public mandate, museums often seek grants for
technology and personnel to digitize their collections and to catalog
and organize the materials for online access. Eppich comments:

> I have said many times here that there is no reason to create
> archives if we don't give the public some access. Public
> access, of course, can be [created through] the technology—
> there's lots of archival stuff out there on the Web. We all just
> have to learn to put the content there, which isn't something
> that museums do on a regular basis.

An example of a museum that has digitized its collections for public
access is the Wisconsin Historical Society, which on their website offers
not only an online catalog of their publication and archival holdings but
other specialized databases such as the Civil War Roster of Volunteers
or the Wisconsin Genealogy Index, which searches vital records (birth,
death, and marriage records) and biographical sketches and news articles.

Whether or not a museum has a librarian and/or archivist depends
on the institution's size, age, collection, and discipline. Small to mid-
sized organizations may not have their own library and will task their

curator or registrar with caring for any archival materials. A museum with a strong collections research component and a long history, such as a historical society that began in 1918, is more likely to have an extensive library and archival collection than a children's museum that originated in 1994. And at certain history institutions like presidential museum and libraries, the archives comprise much of the permanent collection.

Larger museum libraries and archives have staff dedicated to specialties such as photographic collections, reference services, collections management, circulation, journals and periodicals, and book conservation. They may also have archivists dedicated to digital images and records. In terms of hierarchy, librarians and archivists typically fall under the supervision of the collections or information management departments, but they could also be part of the education or curatorial teams.

Career Ladder and Salary Ranges

Librarian assistant: $25,000 to $38,000
Assistant librarian: $30,000 to $40,000
Librarian: $40,000 to $50,000
Visual resources librarian: $40,000 to $60,000
Director/head librarian: $40,000 to $60,000+

Assistant archivist: $25,000 to $45,000
Archivist: $30,000 to $50,000
Chief archivist: $45,000 to $60,000+ (can be more than $100,000 at museums with very large archival collections, such as the National Archives and Records Administration)

Education and Experience

Both of these positions usually require an undergraduate degree in the subject specialty of the museum, and, for librarians, a master's degree in library science (M.L.S.) or in library science and information studies (M.L.I.S.) from a university accredited by the American Library Association (ALA). Pratt Institute in New York offers a museum librarianship certificate as part of their M.L.I.S. degree. And schools such as Indiana University and the University of North Carolina, Chapel Hill, offer dual degree options such as an M.L.S. and an M.A. in art history or music studies, for example. Archivists may have a master's in archival studies, library science, public or oral history, history, or museum studies. Doctorates are required for top positions at major archival collections.

Depending on the position's rank, required experience for library jobs may include at least two years working with catalog databases and software, image collections, and professional cataloging practice. Experience at public or academic libraries is applicable. For archivists, preferred experience includes any positions that involve working with archives or objects within an institutional setting and with cataloging software.

JOB ANNOUNCEMENTS AND PROFESSIONAL DEVELOPMENT

Compared to most museum jobs, the wealth of professional organizations for librarians and archivists is overwhelming. The American Library Association caters to the broad spectrum of library science, whereas the Art Libraries Society of North America (ARLIS/NA) obviously focuses on art and visual resource collections; both have links to job listings. Also see the resources available through the Special Libraries Association, which caters to employees of non-traditional libraries such as museums, colleges, companies, hospitals, etc.

The SAA posts openings for all types of organizations including museums, libraries, universities, civic governments, and corporations. You can also find listings on the website of the National Association of Government Archives and Records Administrators. The SAA also provides opportunities for professional development and training, which is especially important as people in this field may find themselves caring for everything from crumbling old letters to mp3 files. The Academy of Certified Archivists and the Institute of Certified Records Managers both offer certification programs that are not mandatory, but they prove to employers that you have received and maintain training in archival principles and practices and that you are committed to the profession's ethics and standards.

PHOTOGRAPHER

Have you ever wondered how images of artworks or exhibition installations end up in newspaper reviews, advertisements, and even on t-shirts and magnets promoting the museum? The museum photographer is responsible for creating those images, which now are primarily digital, and for storing and cataloging the thousands of photographic records of the museum. The storage function aligns this position with that of archivist and information officer.

Tad Fruits is manager/photographer in the Photography Department at the Indianapolis Museum of Art. He says the department

> is an all-digital photographic studio, serving the historical, archival, and publication needs of the IMA. Digital still documentation is created of the art collections, permanent and temporary exhibition galleries, historic Lilly House, grounds and gardens, as well as educational and special event activities. Our core responsibility is and continues to be the thoughtful documentation of works of art for the purpose of historical record, presentation via electronic and print media, and the planning and creation of collections and exhibition catalogs.

At IMA, the Photography Department resides within the collections support division of the museum, but that can vary depending on the institution and the responsibilities. Some photographers work for registrars; others are supervised by the Marketing Department. Many museums that can't afford in-house photographers hire freelancers or agencies or task other staff members, such as preparators, with the responsibility.

CAREER LADDER AND SALARY RANGES
PHOTOGRAPHY ASSISTANT: $25,000 to $40,000
PHOTOGRAPHER: $30,000 to $50,000

EDUCATION AND EXPERIENCE
An undergraduate degree in the fine arts, with a focus on photography is required. The University of North Texas, Denton, offers one of a growing number of master's degree programs in digital image management through their school of library and information sciences.

JOB ANNOUNCEMENTS AND PROFESSIONAL DEVELOPMENT
The Visual Resources Association and the Museum Computer

Network post listings and provide professional development for this position and jobs related to digital imagery.

PREPARATOR/ART HANDLER

When you enter an exhibition, almost everything around you has been installed, arranged, and possibly even created by a preparator. Preparators don't just prepare objects for display—matting and framing artwork or making mounts for three-dimensional objects—they also install and deinstall entire exhibitions, which includes painting and constructing temporary walls, hanging art or panels on the walls, assembling interactive components and building cases, placing labels and other didactic materials in their proper location, and adjusting lights for maximum effect. And they perform routine maintenance in the exhibition galleries, such as replacing lights, touching up paint, making sure no exhibition components have been broken or damaged, etc. They assist in planning the exhibition's layout within the gallery prior to installation and consult on the exhibition's design and fabrication. They might also photograph exhibition displays for the museum's archives and objects in the collection for the museum's database.

Behind the scenes, preparators pack and unpack objects for shipping or storage, move objects from one place to another (such as from storage to the conservation lab), and in general assist with collections care, which can include cleaning specimens in addition to objects and artifacts. Some preparators have specialties, like working with computer interactives, handling sacred American Indian objects, or making mounts (the armatures that support three-dimensional objects on display, such as jewelry or dinosaur skeletons).

The preparator's job is essential to museums; the larger the museum and the more complicated the exhibitions, the more preparators are needed. At very large institutions, such as the Museum of Modern Art, there are different crews dedicated solely to lighting, painting, moving artwork, or other task-specific responsibilities. When museums work with unusually complex exhibitions, they sometimes hire temporary preparators to assist with installation and deinstallation—this can be a chance for novices to garner experience and make contacts. At smaller institutions, the registrar or curator may also act as the preparator. Senior preparators report to exhibition managers, registrars, or curators.

The ubiquity of the preparator's responsibilities makes it an attractive job for people who want to gain a foothold in a museum and possibly transfer to other object and exhibition-related positions. Also, art and exhibition transport companies like Artex or U.S. Art hire and train preparators for their services to museums. The skills gained from working at one of these companies apply to preparator positions at museums.

CAREER LADDER AND SALARY RANGES

PREPARATOR: $20,000 to $38,000
CHIEF PREPARATOR: $35,000 to $50,000

EDUCATION AND EXPERIENCE

A high school degree or GED is required; an undergraduate degree is an asset, particularly with classes in studio art as well as carpentry, construction, photography, and woodworking. Advanced degrees in museum studies are desirable for senior positions. As a hands-on job, experience working with power tools, manual dexterity, and the ability for heavy lifting and moving may be required.

JOB ANNOUNCEMENTS AND PROFESSIONAL DEVELOPMENT

See AAM's Packing, Art Handling, and Crating Information Network and the National Association for Museum Exhibition.

REGISTRAR/COLLECTIONS MANAGER

As the registrar/collections manager at the Valentine Richmond History Center, Jackie Mullins says that her combination title is pretty common except at larger museums, where

> collections managers are more responsible for the physical object (conservation, storage, inventory, etc.) while registrars are more responsible for intellectual control (anything related to paperwork such as deeds, deaccessions, loans, tracking provenance, etc.).

In a small to mid-sized museum, this position might be called simply "registrar," or the curator might be in charge of object care and record-keeping.

The registrar/collections manager ensures the long-term stability of objects by using proper storage, handling, and maintenance procedures. Often this role involves researching the objects themselves, meaning their chemical and physical makeup along with their history and learning about cool things like mite infestation, how to stop the spread of fungi, the dangers of extreme humidity levels, and what to do when someone donates a collection of rare seashells in the very same potato chip tin that they have been stored in for twenty years. The registrar conducts regular inventories of the storage areas and makes recommendations for object needs, such as conservation or matting and framing repairs.

Using collections management software, this person documents that every object that enters or exits the museum building formally enters the museum's collection, which is called accessioning, is moved on or off display or to the Conservation Department, or is lent out and shipped to another museum. The registrar also maintains records on the object's history (provenance) prior to entering the museum collection, such as previous owners, auction or purchase records, or donor information. Depending on the collection, the registrar records the object's maker and year of origin, its species or other identifying nomenclature, dimensions, insurance value, and exhibition history and its current physical location. The registrar/collections manager creates and inputs digital images of the objects into the database or arranges for the photography needs of the collection.

Registrars/collections managers also help curators and exhibition developers determine what objects would be best suited for display and tell the story of the exhibition. Mullins enjoys working with objects because of their role in material culture. "A person can tell the best story ever, but to have an object to show as a real physical confirmation of that story is fascinating to me." She says that her biggest challenge is

> finding the balance between doing what is right for the objects
> and making them accessible to the public. Every collection has
> at least one or two objects that are phenomenal, but are too
> fragile for exhibition or cannot be studied by researchers—
> these objects lose some of their "value" to the institution.

Registrars also coordinate the physical movement and condition of exhibitions, their furniture (cases, platforms, panels) and the objects included within them. They organize the shipping of exhibitions to and from the institution, oversee packing and unpacking, review exhibition installation, and conduct condition reports on exhibition contents, which means they look for and record any observable damage that occurred during transit or while on view. When shipping particularly precious objects, the registrar may act as a courier and accompany the objects when they travel between destinations.

The position of registrar/collections manager is often included within a curatorial department, with the head registrar reporting to the senior curator. The registrar may supervise the preparators, or, in the case of a small institution, they may also have a preparator's duties.

CAREER LADDER AND SALARY RANGES

REGISTRARIAL ASSISTANT: $20,000 to $35,000

ASSISTANT REGISTRAR: $25,000 to $40,000

REGISTRAR: $30,000 to $45,000

CHIEF REGISTRAR: $40,000 to $60,000+

COLLECTIONS MANAGER: $25,000 to $45,000

EDUCATION AND EXPERIENCE

Preferred education includes an undergraduate degree in the subject specialty of the museum and advanced degrees in museum studies or related fields. Preferred experience includes any positions that involve working with objects and/or exhibitions within an institutional setting. Experience with collections management software, national and international shipping, exhibition fabrication and production, object handling and packing, and the coordination of national and international exhibition tours are necessary for mid- to upper-level positions.

JOB ANNOUNCEMENTS AND PROFESSIONAL DEVELOPMENT

Look for job listings under headings for both registrars and collections managers, and look at AAM's Registrar's Committee and the Packing, Art Handling, & Crating Information Network for listings and continuing education opportunities. Because object care is critical for so many institutions, regional museum associations often offer classes, workshops, and conference sessions on the topic. And see the conservator's position description for additional professional organizations that offer training relevant to registrars and collections managers.

CHAPTER FOUR

JOBS WITH A PUBLIC FOCUS

The jobs in this grouping all have some sort of public dimension to their responsibilities. The education, retail, and security staff interact with on- and off-site visitors daily. The fundraising and marketing personnel promote the museum to people as a way of attracting their visitation and financial support. The editor's and information officer's public is their readership or users, which could be exhibition visitors, scholars, or schoolchildren, to name just a few segments. These jobs are discussed in this chapter:

- **DEVELOPMENT OFFICER/MEMBERSHIP MANAGER**
- **EDITOR**
- **EDUCATOR/VOLUNTEER MANAGER**
- **INFORMATION OFFICER**
- **MARKETING MANAGER/PUBLIC RELATIONS MANAGER**
- **RETAIL MANAGER**
- **SECURITY CHIEF**
- **VISITOR SERVICES MANAGER**

DEVELOPMENT DIRECTOR/MEMBERSHIP MANAGER
(ALTERNATE TITLE: HEAD OF ADVANCEMENT)

The development director initiates and oversees all fundraising activities to ensure that they maximize funds for the museum, follow all laws applicable to nonprofits, and complement the institution's mission. These activities include soliciting individual donors, organizing fundraising galas and benefit auctions, applying for grants from government entities and foundations, running annual fund campaigns, and organizing museum membership campaigns. The development director works very closely with the museum's director, board members tasked with fundraising, as well as staff in marketing and public relations departments to publicize campaigns and produce materials and in education and exhibitions departments to learn what projects need funding and how best to support their initiatives.

Probably the most challenging fundraising activity is a capital campaign, which is a multi-year fundraising project with a predetermined monetary goal, intended for a specific purpose such as paying for a new building or adding to the museum's endowment; these campaigns can also focus on specific curatorial projects, special exhibitions, and/or publications. An endowment is an investment fund that generates interest income for the institution, which is usually overseen by the Finance Department. The development director collaborates with the museum's director and board members to raise these funds from the community or other sources.

The development director works with different departments to create hard copy and virtual fundraising materials, such as newsletters or magazines, invitations, special promotions, the members' website or portal, and e-newsletters. Museums may outsource mass mailings of hard copy materials such as renewal letters, exhibition preview invitations, or general announcements to save on labor costs.

The development staff's most precious tool is their database of information about funders. Larger institutions hire membership or development systems specialists who are responsible for end-user support, systems analysis, security, reporting, programming, and maintenance of all software and hardware used by the membership, development, and possibly visitor services departments, often to generate specific reports to be used for analysis, mailings, etc.

The director of a small museum might be the primary fundraiser, or there may be one development staff member who handles everything from the donation box at the museum's entrance to grant writing to organizing fundraising dinners. At larger institutions, the development director oversees a staff that specializes in specific functions. One group of employees is solely responsible for foundation grants, another for fundraising events such as galas or even facility rentals for private events, one for corporate solicitations, one for individual gifts, and another that runs the membership campaign.

Museum membership is an especially important function of the Development Department because it provides an active link to the local community, generates interest in the museum's activities, and can be a fairly dependable source of unrestricted funds, meaning the money can be spent on anything—electricity, conference fees, office supplies, salaries, etc. In return for an annual fee, museum membership programs offer special benefits like invitations to exhibition previews, discounts on merchandise in the gift shop, and free admission.

The membership manager's primary responsibility is to recruit and retain members. He or she also encourages current members to increase their donation level, join additional museum member groups—such as a Friends of African Art group—contribute to annual funds or capital campaigns, and consider funding other initiatives. Those in senior-level positions work with development and marketing staff on strategic plans to increase the number of members, and membership campaigns are often organized around blockbuster exhibitions with special packages, such as free admission and audio tours for visitors who sign up for membership on the spot. Typically, membership is part of the Development Department, but it may reside within the marketing or visitor services departments instead.

As representatives of the museum, development staff must be extremely knowledgeable and convey excitement about their organization. Ellen Efsic, director of development at the Contemporary Arts Museum in Houston, says, "Convincing someone to invest their time and/or money in the museum is a big, big, big high and it is one of my major motivators. It's really hard to do when you yourself are not passionate about the mission." She also stresses that fundraisers should be proactive, personable, and good with name and face recall because they meet so many people in the course of their workday.

Because the job secures crucial monetary support for the museum, employee retention can be critical, and success is often rewarded financially. Thus, fundraisers tend to be paid more than other museum professions except for directors or other top administrators. Regarding salaries, Annie Elliot, a freelance fundraiser based in DC who has worked for many large art institutions, says, "Especially when you're just starting out, there can be a big difference between earning $20,000 as a curatorial assistant or earning $30,000 in development."

And performance counts; fundraisers with a record of success can find themselves in great demand. But Elliott advises,

> Stay in a decent job at least two years to learn all you can
> before moving around; it looks suspect to have too many

short-term jobs on your résumé. Because good fundraisers are hard to find, you'll have opportunities to jump around more often. Don't do it. You won't get a director of development position anywhere if your résumé shows a series of one-year posts, and you won't be developing your skills as thoroughly as you should.

CAREER LADDER AND SALARY RANGES

DEVELOPMENT ASSISTANT: $25,000 to $49,000
ASSISTANT DEVELOPMENT DIRECTOR: $30,000 to $50,000
DEVELOPMENT DIRECTOR: $45,000 to $75,000
VICE PRESIDENT FOR DEVELOPMENT (at largest museums): $80,000 to $110,000+

MEMBERSHIP ASSISTANT: $21,000 to $35,000
MEMBERSHIP DATABASE ANALYST/SYSTEMS MANAGER: $50,000 to $60,000
DIRECTOR OF MEMBERSHIP: $35,000 to $50,000

EDUCATION AND EXPERIENCE

An undergraduate degree in business, communications, marketing, public relations, accounting, or subject specialty of the museum is required; advanced degrees in business or arts administration are highly valued and may be required for senior-level positions. Any fundraising experience is applicable, but especially that in the arts, museums, and nonprofits; three to five years of experience are required for mid-level and above positions. Experience with fundraising software such as Raiser's Edge or other similar programs may be required.

JOB ANNOUNCEMENTS AND PROFESSIONAL DEVELOPMENT

The *Chronicle of Philanthropy* and the Association of Fundraising Professionals post jobs on their websites. The latter organization offers professional development with classes and conferences and a certification program in fundraising, which is not required by employers but can enhance a candidate's résumé.

Editor

(Alternate Titles Include Writer/Editor or Head of Publications)

As managing editor at the National Museum of Women in the Arts in DC, Elizabeth S. G. Nicholson oversees "everything that appears in print, from the 15-foot-long banner that hangs outside the museum to the smallest postcard we sell in the shop. In between are books, gallery brochures, wall labels, invitations to museum events, and classroom materials for teachers and students." Editors also oversee text for museum websites, e-news, and any other virtual written or promotional material.

When working with freelance or in-house writers or when writing themselves, editors ensure that the text is factually correct, is appropriate for the museum and its audience, and conforms to grammatical and stylistic guides, such as the *Chicago Manual of Style*. Editors are very aware of the intended readers of these written materials, so an exhibition label about a Roman sarcophagus will have very different content and tone than an article about the sarcophagus published in the museum's scholarly journal on ancient art, a paragraph about the acquisition of the sarcophagus in the museum's annual report, or a description of the piece included in the museum's online exhibition about Roman art created for children in 3rd and 4th grades.

The editor also acquires images and copyright permissions for printed matter and collaborates with graphic designers and printers to oversee the production of printed material to ensure that the quality meets the standards of the museum and is produced in a timely manner. This person usually reports to the director of marketing, communications, or external affairs or to the head of publications, a position applicable to museums that publish significant numbers of catalogs, books, articles, and other relevant printed materials. Editors work closely with any department that produces text for public consumption, especially fundraising, education, exhibitions, and curatorial staff.

Editing positions can be found at mid- to large-sized institutions that can afford to produce extensive written and printed material. And although editors can make higher salaries at larger nonprofits or in the private sector, Nicholson says that there are few "better opportunities for producing beautiful and interesting illustrated books, magazines, and other publications. I have met such interesting people and learned so much in this field that I can't imagine wanting to go to work in any other environment."

CAREER LADDER AND SALARY RANGES
EDITORIAL ASSISTANT: $25,000 to $35,000
EDITOR: $30,000 to $45,000
HEAD OF PUBLICATIONS: $45,000 to $65,000+

EDUCATION AND EXPERIENCE
Preferred degrees include a bachelor's degree in English, communications, or journalism, or subject areas related to the museum's discipline. Experience in any type of editorial position is often applicable, including proofreading and copyediting. Applicants must be proficient in various word processing and graphic design software. Classes on professional copyediting are also recommended and are available at colleges and universities.

JOB ANNOUNCEMENTS AND PROFESSIONAL DEVELOPMENT
Museums sometimes list openings on the following websites: mediabistro.com, journalismjobs.com, and publishersmarketplace.com. The University of Chicago's Graham School of General Studies offers a biannual seminar on museum publishing that provides a networking opportunity as well as sessions on everything from online publishing to finding overseas publishers to dealing with troublesome writers.

EDUCATOR/VOLUNTEER MANAGER
(ALTERNATE TITLES INCLUDE CURATOR OR DIRECTOR OF EDUCATION, PROGRAMS MANAGER, OR DIRECTOR OF LEARNING, OUTREACH, OR INTERPRETIVE PROGRAMS)

Educators instigate, facilitate, and expand the museum's educational mission by creating and evaluating opportunities for informal learning (i.e., learning that takes place outside of the traditional classroom environment). Their responsibilities are focused on developing, managing, and assessing the museum's public programs, including tours of exhibitions and galleries, lectures, performances, films, demonstrations, symposiums, internship programs, workshops, school group visits, and field trips.

Educators also write text and design materials to be used by the museum's on- and off-site audiences. Examples include exhibition gallery guides or brochures, children's guides, resource kits that enable school teachers to use the museum's exhibitions and collections in their classrooms, and online didactic materials such as an interactive view of a selection of the museum's collection.

At some museums, such as science centers or children's museums, educators organize exhibitions, from choosing the exhibition theme to picking objects and/or displays to writing label and panel text. Depending on the museum's staff hierarchy, the education office might be the driving force behind the organization's overall programming, meaning it proposes what exhibitions or events will happen in the future to meet specific educational and audience development goals.

The term "audience development" describes the study and cultivation of visitors and/or members to the museum. Educators study the demographics of their museum's audience—on-site, off-site, and virtual—and determine what types of programs will best suit the museum's mission and that audience. Usually, these activities target specific segments of a community. For example, an educator might learn that her or his town has increasing numbers of home-schooled children. Knowing that parents of home-schooled children utilize field trips in their lessons, the educator would work on creating and promoting special activities for these kids using the museum's collections and exhibitions to add another dimension to their learning and to encourage their visitation. The educator could create brochures and a website about home-schooling opportunities, as well as talk about the museum at home-schooling association workshops and meetings.

Some educators act as visitor studies specialists, meaning they are constantly gathering and evaluating information about visitors to ensure that the public is at the center of exhibition and program planning. During exhibition development they contribute ideas on how to best communicate with and interact with visitors, and during production they may test prototypes with different audience segments. Once exhibitions are in place, educators spend time "on the floor" observing foot traffic patterns and audience interaction and asking visitors questions about their backgrounds, their expectations for the exhibition, and the exhibition itself to see if they gleaned the themes and content intended by the exhibition developers. This information is then analyzed and shared with museum staff to improve visitor experience overall and exhibition and project development. Often this evaluative work is conducted in conjunction with the exhibitions and visitor services departments.

Dana Baldwin, the Peggy L. Osher Director of Education at the Portland Museum of Art, Maine, entered the field of museum education to combine her passion for art with teaching. "There are so many things that I enjoy each day at my job," she says,

> and I'm not just saying that to be a Pollyanna. I love it when kids come to the museum, and they have great insight about a work of art. I always remember when a really bright little girl who went to one of our weeklong art camps was explaining Picasso and Cubism to me. She was explaining the way that he took each side of the three-dimensional object and put them all on the same flat plane so that you could study all the dimensions simultaneously. She said, "Look at how he does that. He makes you SEE the FLATNESS." And that really knocked me out. ... And of course, there's the big rush of a really successful program—where 1,000 people come to hear a lecture or something like that. Just the success of that kind of thing is a huge adrenaline pump.
>
> But at this point in my career, I think that interest in a museum as an agent for community change or as an organization that can improve the quality of life in its city is starting to fuel my work as much as interest in teaching people in the traditional sense. I think that stems from being raised in a family of community activists. I wouldn't be able to work in another area of the museum outside of the Education Department.

Educators also supervise and train volunteers, including docents, who are volunteer tour guides. Even the smallest museums—especially the smallest—have many volunteers, sometimes numbering in the hundreds or more. To effectively utilize volunteers, volunteer managers consult with museum staff to learn about tasks that can be completed by volunteers and what sort of training should be provided. They then solicit volunteers through a variety of means, such as the museum's newsletter, website, notices at like-minded community organizations, or word of mouth. At the same time, they oversee the schedules and performance of current volunteers and continue to train those working directly in the Education Department. Although personnel in different departments such as collections or public relations supervise their own volunteers, volunteer managers screen and coordinate their placement. They are responsible for making sure all of the museum's volunteers are treated well and acknowledged for their contributions to the museum.

At a small museum, the curator may also be the organization's primary educator. Medium- to large-sized museums employ many educators who focus on different segments of their audience, such as adults, children, teenagers, families, and senior citizens. Some educators may spend more of their time outside rather than inside the museum, giving lectures and workshops in classrooms, for example. As such, they are the museum's primary liaison with their town's education community, including public and private school systems and colleges and universities. Or their audience may be hundreds or thousands of miles away, thanks to distance learning programs via satellite television or the Internet.

Educators work closely with all of the departments that focus on visitors, including marketing and public relations, fundraising, as well as curators and exhibition managers. They may report to the museum's director or to the person in charge of the museum's public dimension, such as a vice president of external affairs.

Career Ladder and Salary Ranges
Education assistant: $20,000 to $35,000
Volunteer coordinator: $29,000 to $37,000
Assistant education director: $27,000 to $50,000
Director of education: $40,000 to $70,000+
(more than $100,000 for head of public programming at largest institutions)

Education and Experience
An undergraduate degree in education and/or subject specialty of the museum is required. Senior positions require graduate degrees in museum education, museum studies, or education in the museum's discipline, such as arts education. While completing her graduate degree in museum education, Baldwin chose art history classes for her electives, which she says helped her build a knowledge base and vocabulary for her specialty in art museums. Within her Education

Department, she has staff with degrees in art history, American studies, and a Master of Fine Arts, to name just a few.

Preferred experience includes any positions involving education and/or audience development or interaction with visitors, such as being a tour guide. Skills and experience from other nonprofit sectors involving informal learning, such as libraries and the arts, translate to the museum field. Likewise, experience with formal education, such as classroom teaching, is also applicable. A criminal background check may be required for positions that call for interacting with minors or for all educational positions at children's museums and science and technology centers.

JOB ANNOUNCEMENTS AND PROFESSIONAL DEVELOPMENT

See job listings posted on the websites for the AAM's Educators Committee and the Committee on Audience Research and Evaluation, the latter of which focuses specifically on visitor studies. The Museum Education Roundtable is an independent nonprofit organization based in Washington, DC, that publishes the *Journal of Museum Education* with Left Coast Press. Additional opportunities for professional development include associations for subject-specific educators such as the National Art Education Association.

The American Association for Museum Volunteers and the National Docent Symposium Council provide information and professional development for volunteers and their managers.

INFORMATION OFFICER
(ALTERNATE TITLES INCLUDE VISUAL RESOURCES CURATOR OR DIGITAL ARCHIVIST)

As mentioned in Chapter Two on Museum Trends, technology is changing how museums operate, and this is no more apparent than in information management, which has sparked the creation of new positions that meld the responsibilities of librarian, archivist, collections manager, educator, photographer, and registrar. The information officer (IO) works in the field of informatics, which is the collection, classification, storage, retrieval, and dissemination of information via computer systems. The retrieval and dissemination factors define the primarily educational function of the position hence the inclusion of this job with others that have a public focus. Information technology has also transformed museums' retail and ticketing operations through e-commerce and online marketing.

Richard Urban is a doctoral student in the Graduate School of Library and Information Science, University of Illinois at Urbana-Champaign, and a research assistant at the ECHO Depository Project (National Digital Infrastructure Preservation Project). "Since the advent of the Web," Urban says,

> museum informatics has been concerned with sharing information online. However, it also involves all the behind-the-scenes work that goes into responsible collection management. Beginning in the late 1960s, museums began to automate their collection records. Largely this was for internal use only by curators, registrars, etc. The web has put pressure on museums to make more of this information public via the web or other means. Public funding and public grants usually come with stipulations that the information is widely available and not limited to museum staff only. Part of the work is translating information that can be understood by professionals into public-friendly information.

As an example of the complexity involved in informatics, take a look at some of the online projects that won Best of the Web distinction, awarded annually at the international Museums and the Web conference, organized by the Archives and Museum Information association. Awards are bestowed on the best online exhibitions, e-service or e-commerce, research and other categories. Also see The Metropolitan Museum of Art's "Timeline of Art History" on their website, which offers a global, historical, and educational perspective on their permanent collection.

Relatively new to the museum world, this is a particularly lively profession at the moment with many opportunities for creativity and advancement. Regarding career opportunities, Urban says,

> Digital information is now at the core of many museum functions, from collections management, education, member relations, even pest and climate control. In order to make

effective and efficient use of this information, museums need more professionals with skills in information management, who at the same time can appreciate the values we hold as museum professionals.

But will these jobs be around in the next decade or two? Urban responds:

> Technology moves too fast to accurately predict what it will look like in twenty years. However, we already know that we need to look beyond simply curating physical objects and including digital media in our ability to function as keepers of culture. If we want anything that is created digitally today to be around in twenty years, this is a reality we have to face as a profession. Our audiences in the future will also have grown up with complex digital technologies, such as social networking, online video games, etc., and we need to continue adapting our values and goals as a profession to these new mediums. Work in this area is certain to grow, especially for people with the right hybrid of skills as museum professionals and as effective information managers.

The IO's position within the museum hierarchy varies per institution. Urban says,

> Larger museums might have either a Chief Technology Officer (CTO) or a Chief Information Officer (CIO). Collections databases often fall under the registrar's office, and marketing departments frequently manage websites. And libraries are usually their own separate branches of collections departments. It's actually one the challenges of the field that many museums have very dispersed technologies that makes coordination difficult. There has been some recognition that more strategic planning is needed to make all the pieces work together, and there is also a move towards integrating information from across different museums/collections.

CAREER LADDER AND SALARY RANGES
INFORMATION ASSISTANT: $35,000 to $50,000
INFORMATION OFFICER: $70,000 to $95,000+

EDUCATION, EXPERIENCE, AND SKILLS

The preferred education is an undergraduate degree in the subject specialty of the museum and a graduate degree in library science, information science, or information technology. Several museum studies programs offer courses in museum informatics. Depending on the position, required experience can include at least two years working with related databases and software, image collections, and professional cataloging practice. Experience at other institutions, particularly nonprofits such as libraries or universities, is applicable.

JOB ANNOUNCEMENTS AND PROFESSIONAL DEVELOPMENT

As of this writing, there is no online resource of job openings for all types of museum information service and IT positions, but employers do post to the Museum Computer Network (MCN) listserve. And the Visual Resources Association (VRA) posts listings on their website of image management positions at all variety of organizations, especially universities. Urban recommends reviewing openings for registrars/collections managers, as those jobs may include information management duties at smaller museums. MCN and VRA offer networking and professional development opportunities, as does AAM's Media and Technology Committee and the Archives and Museum Informatics association.

MARKETING MANAGER/PUBLIC RELATIONS MANAGER
(ALTERNATE TITLES INCLUDE DIRECTOR OF COMMUNICATIONS, EXTERNAL RELATIONS, OR MEDIA RELATIONS MANAGER)

The primary goal of museum marketing managers is to increase public awareness, on-site and website visitors, sales, and other income to the museum. To fulfill this responsibility, they oversee everything from public relations and advertising to audience research to retail product development. They create short- and long-term marketing strategies to target specific audiences, such as out-of-town tourists or families with young children, as determined by the museum. They may work with the education and exhibitions staff to provide input on what kind of events and exhibitions contribute to the overall profile of the museum and revenue generation. Throughout the marketing projects, they assess progress and alter the activities and plans when necessary to better meet the desired outcomes—all of which are aligned with the museum's mission and its marketing strategy.

Much of the marketing manager's job is devoted to developing, refining, and promoting the museum's brand, which is the public's conception of the institution. Marketing professionals conduct surveys and focus groups to find out what a diverse pool of people in the community think about the museum and whether those responses match the identity that the museum wants to portray.

For example, after surveying a sample of the visiting and nonvisiting public, a marketing manager might find that the history center is perceived as a snooty, dusty center for old papers. A recent grant-funded initiative, however, has enabled the museum to actively focus on engaging young audiences in the excitement of history. To promote this new focus and the museum's commitment to children, the marketing manager will make sure that all forms of the museum's promotions convey this emphasis and energy. For instance, this person will assist educators in publicizing "family fun" days with advertisements and article placements in publications or websites that cater to those audiences. The marketing manager will work with the IT and design departments so that the museum's website can better emphasize children's outreach and accessibility for teachers. The museum will feature photos of children engaged in gallery activities on the covers of history center publications like newsletters or annual reports. The marketing manager might even hire a designer to create a kid-friendly logo or mascot that appears on all printed and digital materials related to the center's programming.

Increasingly sophisticated marketing databases are enabling museums to better track member and visitor information to reach greater numbers of people and to hone their approach. For example, say you buy tickets online to an exhibition on hobbits and you agree to receive promotional information from the museum. When the museum schedules an upcoming show on gnomes, you receive an email saying something like, "If you liked 'Hobbits!' you'll love 'Gnomes!'" And since you bought a ticket for your eight-year-old nephew when you visited the first time, chances are you'll receive emails, mailings, and even coupons for children's programs throughout the year.

At a mid- to large-sized museum, the head of marketing oversees several departments including advertising, sales promotions, public relations, and direct marketing (primarily mailings); they may also work closely with the Communications Department for consistency with the museum's external affairs. A museum may hire an outside advertising or marketing firm for specific projects, such as the promotion of a specially funded blockbuster exhibition or the redesign of the museum's logo. The marketing manager usually reports to the head of operations or the museum director.

At smaller institutions, the museum may not have a marketing manager per se, but they might have a public relations (PR) manager to promote the activities and mission of the institution to the media, which today includes newspapers, periodicals, radio, television, webzines, social networking websites, and blogs. This person's many proactive responsibilities include writing and disseminating press releases and images, courting writers and editors by offering interviews and special tours as well as press conferences, and utilizing the museum's website to garner interest locally and globally. This person may also be tasked with creating and overseeing special events and programming.

The PR manager is the primary point person for press inquiries. When any kind of news is breaking (say controversy over a troublesome board member), the PR manager receives the press calls and emails and then either responds or works with the staff to establish responses. The PR manager also receives requests from publications for images to accompany articles or listings about exhibitions, objects, or people connected to the museum. A PR staffer locates and gathers all articles, listings, and commentaries about the museum that appear in the media to determine future press needs and strategies. And at some museums, this person also promotes the institution to government agencies and officials.

CAREER LADDER AND SALARY RANGES
MARKETING ASSISTANT: $25,000 to $38,000
MARKETING MANAGER: $40,000 to $70,000
HEAD OF MARKETING/COMMUNICATIONS: $60,000 to $80,000+
   (over $100,000 for the largest museums)

PUBLIC RELATIONS ASSISTANT: $25,000 to $45,000
PUBLIC RELATIONS MANAGER: $35,000 to $55,000
PUBLIC RELATIONS CHIEF: $44,000 to $65,000

EDUCATION AND EXPERIENCE

Preferred degrees include a bachelor's in business (advertising, marketing and public relations), communications, or subject areas related to the museum's discipline. A major in English or journalism may be applicable for public relations positions. A graduate degree in business or communications is required for senior-level jobs. Five to seven years of experience creating and implementing marketing strategies is required for advanced positions. Experience with marketing software is desirable.

JOB ANNOUNCEMENTS AND PROFESSIONAL DEVELOPMENT

Because marketing and public relations skills and experience translate to various types of organizations, you'll find museum positions advertised on the following websites: mediabistro.com, PRWeekJobs.com, nonprofit.careerbuilder.com, and workinpr.com. The American Marketing Association and the Public Relations Society of America offers job listings in addition to professional training. AAM's PR and Marketing Committee provides continuing education and networking opportunities.

RETAIL MANAGER
(ALTERNATE TITLES INCLUDE SHOP MANAGER OR PRODUCT AND MERCHANDISE COORDINATOR)

Ka-ching! At many museums, this might be the first sound the visitor hears if not the last one before leaving. Museum stores provide an important source of relatively dependable income in addition to contributing to the institution's public identity in terms of product and service. Museum goers expect the unique experiences offered through exhibitions and programs to be continued in the store, in terms of one-of-a-kind items for sale as well as scholarly publications and quality reproductions.

Shop managers are responsible for stocking the store with goods that will appeal to their visitors, assisting with product development and marketing, ensuring quality customer service among their staff, and overseeing all accounting and logistical needs of the shop. Some museums make their stores destinations in themselves by offering merchandise unavailable anywhere else in town, such as unusual gift items or hard-to-find books.

Large retail operations, like that at the Art Institute of Chicago, have extended beyond the physical site to become multi-million dollar enterprises offering shopping by print catalogs and online. Museums of this size have product and licensing departments that create merchandise specifically for the store highlighting their collections and exhibitions. For example, to coincide with the exhibition "Fierce Friends: Artists and Animals, 1750–1900," the Carnegie Museum of Art in Pittsburgh produced a poster, mug, t-shirt, magnet, and jigsaw puzzle featuring an image of the 1837 painting "The Peaceable Kingdom," by Edward Hicks, from its own permanent collection.

The museum store manager is often part of the museum's Marketing Department, visitor services, or general administration. Small stores might be a one-person or volunteer-run operation; large stores in major cities may employ over 100 people in a variety of full- and part time positions. The notoriously low-paying sales clerk position can sometimes provide entrée into the museum profession for a person who has no previous museum experience. A few of my coworkers at the Smithsonian actually started off as seasonal shop clerks while working toward their undergraduate degrees. When they applied for full-time, professional positions, they'd already been entered into the "system," so to speak, and had solid employment histories with the institution.

CAREER LADDER AND SALARY RANGES
SALES CLERK: minimum wage up to $10/hour,
or $16,000 to $25,000
MANAGER: $30,000 to $45,000
HEAD OF MERCHANDISING/SALES (at largest museums):
$40,000 to $80,000+

EDUCATION AND EXPERIENCE
An undergraduate degree in business, marketing, or accounting is required for most mid- to upper-level positions; graduate degrees are preferred for senior-level positions, particularly for product development. Two or more years of experience in nonprofit retail sales and

management are necessary for advancement, as is supervisory experience.

JOB ANNOUNCEMENTS AND PROFESSIONAL DEVELOPMENT

The primary source for job listings, publications, conferences, etc., is the Museum Store Association, which has established a code of ethics for store personnel available on their website.

SECURITY CHIEF
(ALTERNATE TITLE: HEAD OF PROTECTIVE SERVICES)

Security chiefs are responsible for securing and protecting the museum's building, collections, personnel, and on-site funds such as money from store sales or dining operations, from theft, injury, damage, destruction, and deterioration. They monitor the museum's alarm system, establish and implement emergency procedures, investigate potential criminal activity, coordinate fire department inspections, and ensure that the institution complies with any local, state, or federal safety laws. Depending on the museum, they establish security protocol for staff entering and leaving the building and anyone handling objects of any type, because statistics have shown that employees commit the majority of museum thefts.

Security chiefs hire, train, and supervise the guards—sometimes called museum attendants—who, in many cases, provide the primary contact that visitors have with museum personnel. As such, they are asked a host of questions, from the location of the bathrooms to recommendations for nearby restaurants to explaining whatever it is the visitor is viewing. While acting as on-the-spot concierges and educators, guards mindfully watch and prevent disasters created by curious toddlers tilting toward sculptures, visitors tempted to tap on the reconstructed dinosaur skeleton, and thirsty patrons swigging from hidden cans of soda. The security staff is first to respond and administer first aid in any sort of emergency in the galleries or behind the scenes.

Since 9/11 and Hurricane Katrina, the security industry in general has been tasked with making all public spaces safer—from museums and parks to airports, building lobbies, and mass transit systems. Museum security chiefs work with local emergency response agencies to anticipate and prepare for any potential terrorist act or natural disaster that could gravely affect the museum, its staff, visitors, and collections.

At the smallest museums, the office staff and/or volunteers act as security for the institution. Many large museums contract out security services to professional companies, which, although saving the institution personnel costs, may endanger the high level of customer service assumed by these important public-focused positions. Depending on the museum's location, security guards at the organization might be unionized and include a combination of full- and part-time positions.

The security chief usually reports to an administrator or head of operations. In some cases, security is combined with visitor services. Like the sales clerk position, a job as a museum guard can give you entrée into the institution and provide you contacts. When I volunteered at the Phillips Collection in DC, many of the paid guards were artists, freelance curators, students, and other people interested in learning more about art.

CAREER LADDER AND SALARY RANGES
SECURITY GUARD: minimum wage up to $12/hour
   or $20,000 to $30,000
ASSISTANT DIRECTOR: $25,000 to $40,000
HEAD OF SECURITY: $40,000 to $60,000

EDUCATION AND EXPERIENCE
Entry-level guard positions require a high school diploma or G.E.D. Advanced positions require undergraduate and possibly graduate degrees in criminal justice, public administration, or security management. For upper-level positions, experience in managing a law-enforcement unit or security force is necessary; specialized training in crowd control and cultural property protection is preferred. A criminal background check of new employees may be required.

JOB ANNOUNCEMENTS AND PROFESSIONAL DEVELOPMENT
The International Committee on Museum Security (a committee formed out of the International Council of Museums) addresses security issues and sets standards and vocabularies from a global perspective. In additional to individual museum job postings, these positions can be found on general employment websites such as monster.com, hotjobs.com, and securityjobs.net.

VISITOR SERVICES MANAGER

Since the advent of the blockbuster exhibition—think "King Tut," "Bodies," or anything by the Impressionists—visitor services have become a critical function for museums that lure thousands of people intent on viewing the same exhibition at the same time. A visitor services manager is responsible not only for crowd control but also for ensuring that visitors have a positive and educational experience. This department also gathers information about the visiting public, especially demographics.

To handle large numbers of people, visitor services managers supervise a cadre of staff and volunteers who are responsible for admissions ticketing, parking, audio tours or other interactive guides, visitor information desks, and any other service or product that affects a visitor's experience. The managers also monitor traffic patterns throughout different times of the day and different locations and recommend changes, such as relocating a display of political campaign buttons that causes bottlenecks on the way to the bathroom or shop. Managers train their staff to be a welcoming and helpful presence and to respond to visitor requests and complaints in an obliging manner.

Have you ever been asked for your zip code while you are buying tickets for an exhibition? Visitor services staff administer surveys to the public and compile the data to see if targeted audiences are visiting the museum. The evaluation of that information may take place in this department or in marketing, education, or exhibitions departments where specialists in audience research, learning theory, and statistics also create the questionnaires and survey methodology. The increasing complexity of ticketing, tour group management, and information gathering and analysis has engendered systems or information management positions that focus on the tech end of these visitor services activities.

Usually this position is found at mid- to large-sized institutions whose level of visitation requires a manager. At smaller institutions, this position may not be necessary or its responsibilities may be combined with security, education, marketing, and/or development, specifically membership. Likewise, those in visitor services positions work closely with these departments and are probably overseen by one of them.

When museums ramp up for large-scale temporary exhibitions, they may hire part-time temporary employees to assist with visitor services. These positions, which are often advertised on the museum's website or in local publications, can provide you the opportunity to gain valuable experience in a short amount of time if you are new to the museum profession.

CAREER LADDER AND SALARY RANGES
VISITOR ASSISTANT/FRONT DESK: minimum wage up to $11/hour, or $18,000 to $25,000
VISITOR SERVICES MANAGER: $30,000 to $40,000

EDUCATION AND EXPERIENCE
An undergraduate degree in business (management systems), communications, or education is required for mid-level positions and above; a master's in business or marketing or hotel/restaurant/hospitality is an asset. Leadership positions require at least three or more years of management experience of "on the floor" duties, such as ticketing. Related experience at other institutions such as performing arts centers is applicable. Candidates for jobs compiling data must have extensive experience in relevant computer systems and programs such as C++ applications and Crystal Reports. A criminal background check of new employees may be required.

JOB ANNOUNCEMENTS AND PROFESSIONAL DEVELOPMENT
AAM posts some of the senior-level visitor services positions, but for entry level, check local and national job posting sources (newspapers, craigslist.com, indeed.com) or museum websites. AAM's Committee on Audience Research and Evaluation provides education and professional development for the field of visitor studies.

CHAPTER FIVE

JOBS WITH AN ADMINISTRATIVE FOCUS

The jobs in this section are more likely to be found at larger museums with complex operations involving various revenue streams (e.g., admissions, retail, cafeteria, product development, etc.) or museums with substantial facility maintenance, such as historic houses located on public gardens. At smaller institutions, the director may be responsible for all of the administrative functions of the museum, from budgeting and payroll to housekeeping to computer repair. Positions discussed in this chapter are:

- **ADMINISTRATOR/FINANCE OFFICER**
- **FACILITIES MANAGER**
- **GENERAL COUNSEL/ATTORNEY**
- **HUMAN RESOURCES MANAGER**
- **TECHNOLOGY OFFICER**

ADMINISTRATOR/FINANCE OFFICER

(ALTERNATE TITLES INCLUDE ASSOCIATE DIRECTOR, BUSINESS MANAGER,
DEPUTY DIRECTOR, VICE PRESIDENT OR HEAD OF OPERATIONS,
CHIEF OPERATING OFFICER [COO])

The many meetings, the number crunching, the reports—ah, the glamorous life of an administrator! But even though this is a 100% behind-the-scenes job, the museum administrator's role is crucial to the survival of the organization. This person directs and coordinates practically everything related to the infrastructure of the museum, including money, property, and personnel, as opposed to objects, exhibitions, or education. Responsibilities include managing the following: budgets, event and facility rental, food and retail services, fundraising, grounds and security maintenance, human resources, payroll, legal issues including contracts, marketing and public relations, and visitor services. At large museums, the administrator oversees hundreds of staff with individual departments dedicated to each function mentioned above.

Usually reporting to the director, the top administrator is also involved in the museum's strategic planning, construction projects, and establishing or modifying policies and procedures. This person prepares reports and forecasts for all of these functions to be read and ultimately approved or altered by the director and the board.

Lauren Telchin Katz is a planning specialist in the Office of the Director at the Smithsonian Institution's National Museum of American History. In her job, Telchin Katz says,

> Approximately 50% of my time is spent functioning as an administrator. This entails developing and tracking the museum's evolving strategic plan and ensuring that all plans are consistent with the Smithsonian's goals and priorities. I also serve as the liaison to other offices for the museum director, work closely with the museum's advisory board and serve on the task force for planning the museum's renovation. The rest of my time is spent as a project manager. I recently completed a yearlong project for the museum's reaccreditation self-study with the American Association of Museums. I also spend a great deal of time managing special projects for the director, such as leading a team on redeveloping our website and preparing feasibility studies for museum projects.

Regarding her many duties, Telchin Katz says, "My job is fascinating in that it allows me to interact with every facet of the work at the NMAH. I have a very visible position and as such, I've spent time working with a great array of staff members, ranging from photographers to curators to event planners."

If warranted, a museum may also have a distinct Finance Department or officer who oversees sees the museum's money, assets, and debt—incoming, outgoing, projected, and invested. The finance officer is responsible for ensuring that all of the museum's fiscal and bookkeeping activities comply with legal standards for nonprofits. The director and board regularly call on the officer to produce budgets and statements for review. This person may also manage payroll and benefits and all of the museum's purchasing and service contracts.

Prior to every fiscal year, the finance officer works with department heads to create forecasts and budgets, which are then amended and approved by the institution's director and board prior to implementation. During the year, she or he reviews the figures monthly to monitor spending and income (e.g., ticket sales, memberships) and assess whether they will fall within their projections.

In terms of promotion potential, the senior administrator can be the final step before becoming a director. Whereas in the past curators were groomed to become directors, increasingly complex museum operations have necessitated that a director have business and managerial knowledge and experience. Some museums create two top positions: the executive director, who hails from a more academic or programmatic background, and the CFO, who runs all things administrative under the gaze of the director and board.

Career Ladder and Salary Ranges
Assistant to the director: $30,000 to $45,000
Assistant/deputy director: $45,000 to $75,000
Chief operations officer: $80,000 to $110,000+

Finance assistant: $22,000 to $45,000
Finance/business officer: $50,000 to $85,000+

Education and Experience
An undergraduate degree in business or accounting is preferred; graduate degrees in business, arts management, hotel/restaurant/hospitality management, museum studies, or accounting are required for top positions. Applicable experience Includes project management, nonprofit fiscal management, accounting, bookkeeping, or other administrative roles in arts or other nonprofit organizations. Experience with current accounting software and analysis tools is often required for financial positions.

Job Announcements and Professional Development
See AAM's Museum Management Committee, which unfortunately has no online information at the time of this writing. Otherwise, see postings on websites for nonprofit jobs, such as idealist.org or nonprofit.careerbuilder.com. AAM organizes an annual symposium on current issues in museum management, with several sessions focused on fiscal responsibilities.

FACILITIES MANAGER
(ALTERNATE TITLES INCLUDE SUPERINTENDENT, BUILDING OPERATIONS MANAGER, OR MUSEUM MANAGER)

Who makes sure the lights come on, the toilets flush, the grounds are mowed, and the elevator works? The facilities manager is responsible for maintaining and improving the museum's building and property. As such, this position oversees staff in housekeeping, grounds keeping, telecommunications, protective services, and the physical plant. This manager's crews maintain and provide capital repair (e.g., fixing a leaking roof), oversee the HVAC system (heating, venting, and cooling) and electricity or power systems, offer general carpentry services, and prepare spaces for public events such as lectures, concerts, or opening receptions, and workspaces for the staff, in addition to ensuring that exhibition and storage spaces are safe, secure, and environmentally appropriate for objects and people. Because many of these responsibilities require specialized training or licensed operators, the facilities manager often secures bids from outside contractors, such as plumbers or electricians and is expected to ensure their compliance with building codes and museum standards and review their progress for accuracy, efficiency, and cost.

Facilities managers may also prepare strategic plans, schedules, and budgets for projects involving the facility, such as overhauling an outdated HVAC system or restructuring the museum's entrance to be compliant with the Americans with Disabilities Act. They ensure the museum's structures and operations meet government codes in terms of safety and accessibility. As such, their participation is vital to any plans for museum extensions or major renovations, so they work closely with architects and designers and are often in charge of any contractors, construction crews, engineers, or other personnel involved in those projects.

Facilities managers may manage retail sales, food services, or human resources, or those may be under the purview of the chief of operations, to whom he or she reports. They also work with exhibitions managers, preparators, and registrars when they are installing or deinstalling exhibitions or moving collections objects. Facilities managers oversee any type of machinery in the museum, including everything from copiers to cash registers to trucks and forklifts. They are also responsible for the identification and disposal of hazardous materials and general workplace safety issues, and along with the Security Department they develop emergency preparedness plans.

This position often requires people who are flexible and understand that they may be called in at a moment's notice for immediate repairs or concerns, such as a broken humidity control system or a newly discovered leaking pipe above the painting storage area. Their employees and contractors may be unionized and their working hours might be different than that other museum staff. Facilities managers must be able to provide oversight under tight deadlines and make sure all overtime required of their employees is legal and appropriate to their projects.

CAREER LADDER AND SALARY RANGES
ASSISTANT FACILITIES MANAGER: $20,000 to $45,000
HEAD OF FACILITIES: $38,000 to $55,000+
(over $70,000 at the largest museums)

EDUCATION AND EXPERIENCE
An undergraduate degree in engineering, management, or architecture is preferred; graduate degrees in business, engineering, nonprofit management, or museum studies are required for top positions. Extensive experience in trades such as construction management can replace some educational requirements. HVAC knowledge and supervisory experience is necessary for top jobs. Experience at similar organizations such as universities or performing arts complexes is applicable.

JOB ANNOUNCEMENTS AND PROFESSIONAL DEVELOPMENT
The International Association of Museum Facility Administrators offers conferences, a newsletter, job listings, and an annual benchmarking survey that allows members to compare everything from custodial costs to levels of electricity used per square meter to the number of museums that have implemented disaster recovery plans. Because of the nature of this work, also check local and national sources for job listings as well as websites like engineerjobs.com.

GENERAL COUNSEL/ATTORNEY

Although only the largest institutions can afford or need to have attorneys on staff, working for a museum can be an alternative for someone wanting to escape or avoid the typical legal career path. The general counsel oversees all the legal aspects of a museum's operations, policies, and finance and provides legal advice to the museum's director and board regarding these matters. Examples of responsibilities include contracts, copyright, human relations, planned giving such as trusts and wills, provenance and endangered species issues, risk management, taxes, and compliance with national and international law as it applies to museums and nonprofits.

Some of these topics are specific to museums, but experience and skills gained from other nonprofit institutions are applicable to this position, such as large libraries or library systems, universities, and government agencies. General counsels' offices also include support staff such as administrative assistants and legal assistants, which can provide experience for people interested in this profession but who do not possess law degrees. The museum's top attorney reports directly to senior museum staff, most often the director.

CAREER LADDER AND SALARY RANGES
GENERAL COUNSEL ASSISTANT: $35,000 to $50,000
GENERAL COUNSEL: $75,000 to $110,000+

EDUCATION AND EXPERIENCE

A law degree from an accredited law school and active membership in the bar in the museum's state are required. For a senior position, candidates should have ten or more years of experience dealing with issues specific to nonprofits.

JOB ANNOUNCEMENTS AND PROFESSIONAL DEVELOPMENT

For job listings, consult websites for legal jobs in all fields, such as attorneyjobs.com and lawjobs.com. Law students can inquire with museums or agencies about training opportunities, such as the Institute of Museum and Library Services, which has a legal internship program in their office of the general counsel. Each year, the American Law Institute and American Bar Association host a seminar "Legal Issues in Museum Administration," which provides all museum professionals—not just attorneys—with the latest legal changes affecting the industry.

HUMAN RESOURCES MANAGER
(ALTERNATE TITLES INCLUDE PERSONNEL OFFICER OR DIRECTOR)

Large museums have their own human resources departments to oversee hiring, recruitment, salary, and benefits. Their responsibilities may vary depending on the institution's discipline. For example, at children's museums or museums run by government agencies, background checks may be mandatory for new employees. Human resource managers also ensure compliance with federal and local mandates and agencies such as the Equal Opportunity Commission.

Human resources managers assist in any restructuring of the museum's hierarchy and establishing personnel policies, procedures, and an overall strategic plan, while also providing information and forecasts of salary and benefits costs to administrators for their budgeting and reporting needs. They help department heads with employee relations, grievances, and complaints, and assist in providing professional development and training opportunities for the museum's staff. They also work with IT/information service to ensure that all human resources data and systems are functioning and secure. The senior human resource manager usually reports to the museum's head of administration, operations, or the finance officer.

Some major institutions contract headhunters when trying to fill their top positions. These agencies provide entrée into sectors that the museum may not be familiar with, such as business administration or marketing. They work with the museum's board and Human Resources Department to negotiate salary and benefits packages to lure top candidates.

CAREER LADDER AND SALARY RANGES
HUMAN RESOURCE MANAGER: $42,000 to $63,000
HEAD OF PERSONNEL: $55,000 to $75,000+

EDUCATION AND EXPERIENCE

An undergraduate degree in business, accounting, behavioral science, or liberal arts is required; an M.B.A or M.A. in personnel management may be required for senior-level positions at larger organizations. You can find these programs on the website for the Society for Human Resource Management (SHRM). Some senior-level positions may require certification in human resource management, which can be acquired through local colleges and universities or through the Human Resource Certification Institute (HRCI) and SHRM. Preferred experience includes any type of nonprofit human resource management as well as in computer software such as the Human Resource Information System.

JOB ANNOUNCEMENTS AND PROFESSIONAL DEVELOPMENT

SHRM and HRCI list job openings and offer a variety of professional development programs on their websites. Also look for jobs on general employment websites like monster.com and indeed.com.

TECHNOLOGY OFFICER
(ALTERNATE TITLE: DIRECTOR OF INFORMATION TECHNOLOGY)

Technology officers are responsible for budgeting, acquiring, implementing, and maintaining the equipment and software to support the tech needs of the entire museum. Chief technology officers (CTOs) oversee the planning, installing, maintaining, and managing the museum's computer network, including its security and physical care, such as housing the servers in environmentally controlled areas that are accessible to only a few designated staff. In addition to the network, they are responsible for all computer hardware and accessories used by the staff, including the retail and food services departments, and by the public in exhibition interactives, unless the latter are cared for by the Exhibitions Department.

At smaller museums, this position may be combined with the office manager or facilities manager's job, meaning this person also oversees all additional electronic equipment such as copiers and fax machines as well as telecommunications. At large organizations, the CTO oversees a department of specialists who respond and attend to these various functions, such as network security, digital image management, or "help desk" queries. This position reports to a top administrator, chief of operations, or the information officer.

Career Ladder and Salary Ranges
Technology assistant: $30,000 to $50,000
Chief technology officer: $50,000 to $70,000+

Education and Experience
A bachelor's or associate degree in computer science or information technology is required for entry-level positions; graduate degrees in the same fields are required for advanced positions. Tech experience in any sort of nonprofit sector is applicable.

Job Announcements and Professional Development
With one foot in the tech world and one in museums, these positions are often advertised in local publications and websites such as Craigslist, as well as websites like nonprofitoyster.com. And some jobs are posted on the listserve for the Museum Computer Network. TechSoup.org offers info and training opportunities for people working in the technology field in nonprofits. Also see AAM's Media and Technology Committee and the Archives and Museum Informatics association.

CHAPTER SIX

THE DIRECTOR

Museum directors are hired by the organization's board of trustees to implement their directives and to oversee the museum's financial security and operations. As such, they act as conduits between the board and the staff, regularly reporting to the trustees all progress and changes in the museum's operations and communicating the board's goals, strategies, and policies to the museum workers. At museums without boards, such as some university galleries or government-run museums, directors are usually overseen by an administrative office within the parent organization as well as an advisory committee.

But the director's position is hardly a passive one, as reflected in the increased use of the title of chief executive officer (CEO), which connotes a closer link to business models than academic ones—meaning less scholarship and more money management. Today, museum CEOs and directors provide critical leadership and vision, which in some cases means rescuing the institution from financial ruin or stagnant operations; in other cases, it means building on the successes of the past to become an ever more vibrant and vital organization.

To help me discuss the job of museum director, I interviewed the following people:

1. **SARAH CLARK-LANGAGER, PH.D.,** DIRECTOR OF WESTERN GALLERY AND CURATOR OF OUTDOOR SCULPTURE COLLECTION, WESTERN WASHINGTON UNIVERSITY, BELLINGHAM

2. **VERNON S. COURTNEY, M.ED.,** DIRECTOR OF HAMPTON UNIVERSITY MUSEUM, VIRGINIA

3. **HEATHER FERRELL, M.A.,** DIRECTOR/CURATOR, SALINA ART CENTER, KANSAS

4. **D. D. HILKE, PH.D.,** PRESIDENT/CEO, THE CHILDREN'S MUSEUM OF UTAH AND DISCOVERY GATEWAY PROJECT, SALT LAKE CITY

5. **Chuck Howarth, M.S.**, vice president, Gyroscope, Inc., and former president and ceo of Liberty Science Center, Jersey City, New Jersey

6. **Adam Lerner, Ph.D.**, executive director of The Lab at Belmar, Colorado

7. **Juanita Moore, M.A.**, president and ceo, Charles H. Wright Museum of African American History, Detroit

8. **Terrie S. Rouse, M.P.S. and M.A.**, ceo for visitor services, Capitol Visitor Center, U.S. Capitol, Washington, DC

9. **Walter R. T. Witschey, Ph.D.**, director, Science Museum of Virginia, Richmond

Leadership and Vision

A museum director must be able to identify and anticipate current and future needs of the museum and establish goals based on those needs, especially in terms of its financial stability and growth and its relationship to the community. To create and modify this strategic plan, Terrie Rouse says it is critical to work with the staff and board to

> figure out the common language, so to speak, of the museum. When you can put on paper *who* you are, then you can figure out where the museum needs to go. And every decision the museum makes from that point on is based on the policies you've established for your institution's growth. A good CEO is always assessing and translating the plan by way of the museum's operations.

Chuck Howarth's interest in strategic planning eventually propelled him into consulting after serving for eight years as director of the Liberty Science Center.

> I was and am passionately interested in the next generation of science museums—how can we be more effective as

educators and champions of lifelong learning? When I arrived we had a very effective fundraising board in place, and general agreement that Liberty would be an interactive science center, but no specific plan for what that meant, or what kinds of exhibits and programs Liberty would offer. I spent most of my tenure at Liberty developing and implementing strategies to answer those questions, and thoroughly enjoyed every minute (well, almost every minute.) As Liberty got closer to opening, I realized that the part of the job I love is the strategic planning and program development, and not the headaches (as I perceived them) of running a large organization.

Adam Lerner has the unique experience of literally inventing the museum that he now directs, and it was his vision that convinced a funder to bring his ideas to fruition. While working in the Education Department of the Denver Art Museum, Lerner says, "One day, a patron came to the art museum looking to create a small satellite of the museum at his new development five miles from downtown Denver. I gave him a big proposal for an international contemporary art institution and he bought it." Today, Lerner's main challenge is to "take The Lab from an institution guided by one person's vision (my own) and a single major source of support (the developer) to an organization with an institutional vision and stable, diversified support."

D. D. Hilke spent much of her first year as director of the Children's Museum of Utah as the organizational architect, so to speak, to establish the infrastructure of her greatly expanded staff and facility. "Now," she says,

> I'm much less involved in the day-to-day operations. I'm more like the navigator, ensuring that what we do is part of our mission. But every once in a while I'll take off my president's hat and bring in my exhibitions experience if I'm worried that a project is headed in a wrong direction or if there's no safety net. But otherwise, I step back and let the staff do their work.

BOARD COMMUNICATIONS

Although the director has as many bosses as there are board members, it is often the director who is essentially leading the board, presenting strategies, motivating trustees to approve and be involved in achieving new goals, and even identifying and attracting new board members. Thus, successful museum directors establish mutually beneficial relationships with the organization's board members. When conflicting opinions arise between the director and the board, the director should be able to assist with consensus building while also protecting the interests of the museum—its collections, the public it serves, the programs it offers, and the staff. Rouse says,

> There are no secrets to good board communications. It's your responsibility to provide them with good information so they can analyze it and make decisions. This means you need to get the material out to the board in advance of meetings and vet some ideas over the phone or in person. You do have to deal with a variety of personalities, and sometimes that works fine and sometimes it doesn't. But you have to be a professional and figure out how to make it work.

Vernon Courtney's ten years of working in higher education prior to his museum career provided him with valuable experience in board relations.

> My first rule is candor from the beginning. Whenever an issue clearly becomes something the board must deal with I try to give them complete and early information. This is particularly important if issues hold potential for negative outcomes. While this tact often creates rocky roads for short periods of time it goes far toward fostering trust and allows members to feel comfortable being candid themselves.

"My second rule," Courtney continues,

> is to identify the board members who are most in tune with my philosophical positions, and I try and pay special attention to them early on. Like any other group dynamic everyone isn't always on the same page but an administrator needs to be

aware of who is likely to support you more often than not and who may be a challenge.

OPERATIONS

At many museums, directors oversee staff management, budgeting, and programs, including curatorial and educational activities. They report these activities to the board and work with them to set priorities for the future. As director of the Science Museum of Virginia, Walter Witschey says, "My time is involved in fundraising (25%), board communication (10%), and line management of the museum (65%). These estimates are very rough, and change dramatically week-to-week."

Examples of duties that fall under "operations" at a small museum could include everything from supervising staff and issuing payroll to exhibition planning to managing the facility. The larger the institution, the more duties are delegated to additional staff, and the director can spend more time on evaluation and planning, such as determining if the new membership campaign has successfully increased revenues or if recent educational programs are improving visitor demographics.

As director of the Western Gallery at Western Washington University, Bellingham, Sarah Clark-Langager is one of only two permanent, full-time positions. As typical of small museums, she says,

> I am directly involved in every minute detail. I have to give 100% to all areas. The most challenging is to rise above the competition from other disciplines for the same pots of community money. Given I have to do everything, even my own secretarial work, I wish I had time to write more essays and to curate more exhibitions.

At his previous post—director of the National Afro-American Museum and Cultural Center in Wilberforce, Ohio—Courtney had an operations manager on his staff that allowed him to focus less time on day-to-day operational oversight and more on exhibition and curatorial activity. Larger museums often have a deputy director or chief financial officer dedicated to the financial and administrative functions, who works with the director who can then focus more on overall institutional leadership.

Fundraising

The role of fundraiser consumes a large percentage of many museum directors' workload, due in part to decreasing public funding and increasing operational and programmatic costs. Working closely with the museum's development director and designated board members, directors lead fundraising efforts for major projects such as a new building or increasing the museum's endowment. At small museums, they may also oversee grant activities, membership, and special events like benefit galas.

At her museum in Salina, Kansas, Heather Ferrell says that much of her institution's funding comes from individual donors as opposed to grants. She enjoys development work because:

> At its purest form fundraising is about building relationships with people and the opportunity to share your vision and potential about the institution with others. That is what satisfies me. However, in a town like Salina of 45,000+ people you cannot come in from the "outside" and hope to raise money in a community without respect and a community connection, and that [connection] is my development director.

Juanita Moore says:

> Fundraising forces you to be creative. You have to figure out how to make your museum important to other people, and how to handle hearing "NO!" But you can't let that define you. Rejection really makes you listen to what other people are saying about your museum, creating the opportunity for growth and change. To be successful, you have to be flexible and believe in the power of your product. If not, the funder will know it pretty quickly.

Hilke wishes she'd gained more fundraising experience throughout her career:

> I think not having it prior to my current job held me back from a few positions. I met a lot of people who liked my program experience and credentials but not having development work

was a problem. And I've thought at times it would have been great if I'd gotten an M.B.A., but I just never had time. I seem to always be working on one nearly impossible project or another—so there was never time for another degree.

EXTERNAL RELATIONS AND COMMUNITY ENGAGEMENT

The museum director is the chief spokesperson for the museum. As a figurehead and ambassador, Rouse says, "You're more than just a communicator for your staff and board. You're a symbol of the health of your organization." The director constantly advocates for and increases the recognition of the organization to its various constituencies, meaning members, visitors, the general public, government leaders, the press, and especially potential donors. This is accomplished by being an active member of the local community, serving on public commissions, meeting regularly with the local media, and generally being visible and accessible.

For a museum to succeed, Hilke says,

> Everyone has to understand why the community needs the museum. If the museum were to burn down tomorrow, what would people miss? If the museum isn't an essential part of your community's and of the educational infrastructure of your state, then the museum will have difficulty receiving support. As president of that organization, you have to show that the museum is more than just a destination for visitors—it needs to be an important part of what the city, county, and state aspire to become and promote.

In terms of public involvement, Moore says that a number of cities position their cultural venues to be

> anchors of community revitalization projects. As such we feel obligated to continuously demonstrate our worth and impact. Public involvement and support are central to the success of the museum. The truth is museums need to reflect the voices of the community.

Moore also establishes links to the community through her staff and collections. "As a director in an African American museum, it's really important to help people grow within the field. It's crucial to hire local people to staff the museum because then the community sees itself as participating in the growth that the organization can bring to the area." Moore has also been actively involved in soliciting donations of artifacts and documents related to the museum's mission.

> It's important that the community and general public see that the museum tells their stories, with their voices, and with their things. Strategically it is a great opportunity to educate a wide range of people about the importance of donating to museums the artifacts that help tell their stories. You really need to have broad support to form an institution like this that is people-centered.

EDUCATION AND EXPERIENCE

Consistent with recent hiring trends, the directors interviewed for this book had varied career paths. Moore followed a more traditional route, beginning as a curator at the Ohio Historical Society where she utilized her master's degree in history.

> I spent hours and hours in the "stacks" for weeks at a time, reading and learning about everything they had in the collection on blacks in Ohio. I would volunteer to catalog parts of the collection so I could learn about it, and I traveled around the state to different sites that used the collections.

Howarth entered the museum field as a science educator at the Museum of Science in Boston. "Over the next decade I was fortunate enough to move through a series of positions at the museum, including exhibit development, outreach education, and eventually management, ending up as associate director for education and exhibits." In 1987, Howarth became director of the Liberty Science Center and left that museum in 1993 to join a museum development and design firm. "As I sometimes tell clients," he says, "I have been on their side of the table and have grappled with the same issues they are facing."

In 1980, Witschey was working at The Computer Company, a company he cofounded, when he volunteered to create a special sundial for the Science Museum of Virginia. "While building the dial, I rather casually said to Paul [Knappenberger, then director of SVM], 'You have an interesting job. If you ever leave, let me know.'" Witschey continued volunteering for the museum until 1985, when he left to pursue graduate studies in Maya archaeology at Tulane University in New Orleans.

> As I was completing my degree in 1991, a call came from Richmond that Paul was leaving the Science Museum to become director of the Adler Planetarium. I applied for the job, which required a Ph.D. that I had just completed, and in 1992 became the second director of the Science Museum of Virginia. Although I had volunteer experience of great value, my first museum job was as CEO of the Science Museum of Virginia.

JOYS AND FRUSTRATIONS OF BEING A DIRECTOR

For Rouse, the position of museum director involves a marriage of informal education and analytical work. "I like how the museum field involves philosophical issues as well as the opportunity to excite people." She also enjoys the intellectual stimulation of the job, especially in terms of discovering how to engage people with objects and information. But she also finds that she is often brought in as an instigator at an institution. "As a change agent you are always the target, and sometimes I don't like that."

As a scholar and writer, Lerner found that he has little time to write while simultaneously planning and running a museum.

> There is a great deal I didn't anticipate. As a curator and educator, I had experience with exhibitions, and I had a vague idea about membership and development, but I didn't realize the levels of expertise required for all the other big and small aspects of the institution, including governance (board relations), strategic planning, legal issues, human resources, operations, accounting, community relations, marketing, etc. I underestimated how much time it would

take to manage these aspects of the institution and the costs associated with them.

Regarding museums as a holistic and active organization, Moore says, "I see museums as giants with huge 'voices.' They are major impact players in shaping people's worldviews, therefore there is a tremendous need to be inclusive." As a director, however, Moore says,

> You miss some of the fun. You have less and less time to be directly involved. You have input, but you don't get to be in the "mix" of the programs. Instead you have to learn to listen to other people and delegate otherwise you won't get every-thing done. I tell people that they think being a director means you are in charge. But actually, it means you have more people than ever in charge of you!

A common issue among museum directors is their grueling workload and schedule, which often extends into evenings and weekends with events, meetings, and attempts to catch up on specific projects. Witschey says,

> All the museum directors I know consider their jobs to be 24/7. As a consequence, we tend to be rather near our cel phones and laptops. This is perhaps the modern version of the old system in which the museum director lived on site. Donors and patrons now use email and cel phones too, and they com-municate when it is convenient for them. One of my major donors is notorious for 2:00 am messages—which I seldom see until 5:30 am!

To maintain a work/life balance, Witschey establishes times with his family in which the museum is not a priority and he takes vacations long enough to decompress.

SALARIES AND JOB ANNOUNCEMENTS

Directors of the largest and/or wealthiest museums in the United States command handsome six-figure salaries. On their 2005 IRS form

990, the Kimbell Art Foundation in Fort Worth, Texas, reported a salary of $591,000 for their museum director. In fiscal year 2006, the president of the Museum of Science in Boston received a salary of almost $350,000, and in FY 2004, the executive director/CEO of the Chicago Historical Society received $220,000. At these types of institutions, benefits to directors may extend beyond health care and retirement packages to include expense accounts (almost $250,000 for the director of The Metropolitan Museum of Art in 2004), as well as free housing (large homes in which to entertain donors) and promised bonus packages contingent on certain predetermined financial and expansion goals established by the board. In 2000, Peter C. Marzio, director of the Museum of Fine Arts, Houston, received a staggering bonus of over $1.5 million for successfully generating funds for a major new building in addition to greatly increasing the donations of artwork and money to the museum.

However, the majority of the country's museums do not fall within this elite category. See Appendixes One and Two for some salary averages for museum directors and note that salaries rise in relation to the institution's overall budget. The numbers range from just over $21,000 for a museum in New England with an annual budget under $50,000 to an average salary of over $215,000 reported by the Association of Art Museum Directors (AAMD), whose member organizations must have budgets of $2 million or more. In general, the associations report salaries between $50,000 and $125,000.

Many nonprofit organizations hire their CEOs on a contractual basis, which allows leeway both for the director and the organization to evaluate the quality of leadership, to adjust salary and benefits packages depending upon performance, or to terminate the director if necessary. AAM's online Information Center links to resources for CEO contract negotiation, and AAMD has published a sample museum director's employment contract.

PROFESSIONAL DEVELOPMENT

The Getty Trust's three-week Museum Leadership Institute provides directors and senior museum officials training in management, strategy, and critical thinking skills. Based in Los Angeles, they also offer shorter seminars on topics such as "Museum Leaders: the Next Generation" or "To Be a Director?" The Southeastern Museums

Conference offers the annual Jekyll Island Museum Institute, an eight-day program on management training, on Jekyll Island, Georgia. The Seminar for Historical Administration, offered annually by the American Association for State and Local History, addresses topics such as trustee relations, financial management, managing change, and historic preservation and interpretation. All three of these programs have competitive application processes.

Resources are also provided by the Association of Art Museum Directors. Likewise, the Association of Science Museum Directors offers programs, networking, and educational opportunities. AAM, as well as regional and discipline specific museum associations, also provides conference sessions and seminars for directors.

In addition to attending museum-focused workshops and conferences, Moore reads a wide range of publications on leadership and business, including the *Harvard Business Review*. She says,

> You still look for resources in the museum field, but in order to grow the institution, you need to look to other nonprofit and business sectors to expand your thinking about fundraising, programming, service, and audience development. Then you can see how what others are doing can be applied and expanded upon for your institution. Because the cutting edge developments in leadership and management occur in many fields, you look everywhere, being open to everything.

Ferrell stresses the importance of developing a mentor relationship.

> I am very fortunate to have found a mentor at different points of my career. I have one right now and could not be where I am today without a mentor's insight and shared experience. You should also develop a supportive community of practice. Early on in my career I became active in professional development groups, such as the Western Museums Association, and it is through the wonderful colleagues I met there, as well as from all over the country, that I have learned so much and in turn, felt the confidence to have pursued the position of director. And I love it.

PART THREE
PREPARING FOR AND GAINING MUSEUM EMPLOYMENT

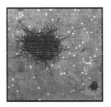

PART THREE
PREPARING FOR AND GAINING MUSEUM EMPLOYMENT

As said before, there is no one ideal route to working in museums. This section of the book details several options for you to consider, including educational choices, internships and volunteer opportunities, and advice for applying for jobs. Like many specialized professions, museums have their own set of criteria when selecting applicants. This can be daunting if you are new to the field, so the advice below is intended to shed light on things that many museum employers look for when reviewing candidates. Note that specific institutions, schools, websites, and programs mentioned in this section are cited as examples and should not be considered as endorsed by myself or Left Coast Press.

Do not limit yourself to the suggestions that follow. Always talk about your goals and solicit assistance from people you meet who know about the museum industry. That could mean professors, supervisors, peers, or anyone else familiar with the job search process and the profession. When I was an intern at a museum at the Smithsonian Institution, I showed my supervisor a job application that I'd filled out for a full time job at another Smithsonian agency. She basically sat me down and explained that little of what I'd written would be sufficient for people in the human resources office to use as I hadn't clearly explained my museum experience and how it related to the open position. With her help I rewrote my application, was called in for an interview, and landed the job—none of which, I'm sure, would have happened if she hadn't assisted me.

CHAPTER SEVEN

EDUCATION

All but a few museum jobs require undergraduate degrees, and many require graduate degrees to advance beyond entry- and mid-level positions. For degree requirements for museum jobs with specialized training, such as archivists and conservators, see the position descriptions in Part Two.

UNDERGRADUATE DEGREES

Almost any undergraduate major is applicable for museum work—even physical education if you consider museums and exhibitions dedicated to sports! For many entry-level museum positions, an undergraduate degree in the liberal arts from a reputable school is more important than majoring in a specific subject because the employer wants to hire someone who is a responsible person, a critical thinker, and a good writer and communicator. Common majors among museum employees include:

- **LIBERAL ARTS TOPICS SUCH AS ART HISTORY, SCIENCE, OR HISTORY, WHICH PARALLEL MUSEUM DISCIPLINES;**
- **ENGLISH;**
- **EDUCATION;**
- **COMMUNICATIONS;**
- **BUSINESS;**
- **STUDIO ART, GRAPHIC DESIGN, ARCHITECTURE/INTERIOR DESIGN;**
- **INFORMATION TECHNOLOGY; AND**
- **SPECIFIC SKILL-RELATED DEGREES, SUCH AS HORTICULTURE, CARPENTRY, ETC.**

Few undergraduate programs offer majors in museum studies or museum-specific disciplines. Some exceptions include Baylor University in Waco, Texas, and other schools such as Southeast Missouri State, Cape Girardeau, which offers a B.S. in historic preservation, and Western Michigan University, Kalamazoo, which offers a B.A. in public history—the study, interpretation, and teaching of history in nonacademic settings. Moore College of Art and Design in Philadelphia recently inaugurated a B.F.A. degree in curatorial studies, which includes a required minor in studio art. Southern Illinois University in Carbondale, Michigan State University in East Lansing, and Brigham Young University in Salt Lake City, along with many other universities, provide minors, areas of concentration, or certificates in museum studies to undergraduates. You can find a listing of undergraduate museum studies programs on a section of the Smithsonian Institution's Museum Studies website that is dedicated to professional development (see Appendix Three for website addresses).

At the University of Richmond, where I work, students can enroll in an area of concentration called "arts management." Arts management focuses on the business of running cultural nonprofit organizations in general, including theaters, orchestras, ballet troupes, cultural art centers, and museums. At Richmond, the program includes one or two museum studies classes per academic year.

Beyond having a degree, competitive job candidates should also have relevant work experience, which engenders the classic college graduate's catch-22—how can you gain experience if you can't land a job that requires experience? To break that cycle, take the initiative during your college years to start filling your résumé with internships, paid or volunteer work, and independent studies that relate to the museum field. For internships and volunteering specifics, see Chapter Nine, but, in general, seek out these opportunities during the school year and summers if financially possible. At the very least, try volunteering one afternoon or morning a week simply to make contacts at the local museum and to find out if you actually like museum work or not.

If your university has a museum, ask about being involved with any of their operations. At our museum, we hire students to run the information desks and act as security during open hours. Once students have proven their reliability, maturity, and interest in museums, we ask them to apply to work with us "behind the scenes" on projects ranging from giving exhibition tours to co-curating exhibitions to designing marketing campaigns for our student body.

Any time you have the opportunity to choose a topic for a class research paper or project, try to relate it to an object in a museum. For example, if you are studying the women's voting rights movement, find out if the local historical society has letters or artifacts relating to suffragettes from the region. Scholars and students are particularly welcomed by museum staff to learn more about objects in the collection. We've had students arrange entire independent study or senior thesis projects around segments of our collections, such as fluorescent rocks or German Expressionist prints. When you ask the museum curator or collections manager to view an object up close or study the object's records and history, you are networking with the local museum community.

If you attend a school in a remote location or if you take night classes because you work during the day, try focusing on an object or theme explored on the museum's website. You can still email the museum staff to learn more about the topic. And, most importantly, don't forget to thank your museum contacts for their assistance and offer to share your findings. Your research may enter the object's records to help future scholars, and it can be used as a means of demonstrating your interest in the museum when you later apply for a job.

Other ways to involve museums in your studies include observing or volunteering to assist with a museum's public relations campaign as a project for your marketing class or training to become a docent for grade school children to apply and evaluate learning strategies that you studied in your education classes.

Ask your professor and/or advisor for ideas, assistance, and museum contacts. If she or he has none, call or email museums yourself. Often, the museum's Education Department is the primary contact with college students, particularly with internships or volunteer projects, but not necessarily with research, which could be organized through the Curatorial Department.

GRADUATE DEGREES

Whereas undergraduate degrees provide you with a strong base of knowledge, graduate degrees can propel you into your career of choice. And progressing straight from undergraduate to graduate school can be an effective and efficient path to museum work as many graduate programs, in addition to providing essential education and training, offer internships and other opportunities to gain access to future employers. But working in a museum prior to acquiring a graduate degree assists you in determining your focus. After I received my B.A. in art history, I was hired as a receptionist at the Contemporary Arts Museum in Houston, deliriously happy to be employed. A few months later I was promoted to being the development office's assistant, where I stayed for three years. The experience taught me incredibly valuable fundraising skills that I still use and convinced me that my future should be in exhibitions and not development. I subsequently enrolled in George Washington University's graduate program in art history.

It is possible to succeed in the museum field without a graduate degree, and you may find this to be true largely outside of cities and other locations where there are concentrated numbers of museums. I'm not suggesting that museums in less-populated areas are not as sophisticated as those in urban ones, but rather that competition for jobs is fiercer in locations with several museums. So would-be employees need to accrue as much education, training, and contacts as they can to join the profession and move up the career ladder.

Generally, museum professionals must amass several years of experience to substitute for a secondary degree. These individuals, though highly qualified, may still find themselves at a disadvantage competing with other job applicants that possess both degrees AND experience.

Publications such as *Peterson's Graduate Schools in the U.S.* can help you identify universities to investigate further at each institution's website. When considering a graduate degree, find out if the school provides opportunities for museum experience through internships or research projects. If not, look up museums in the same location and contact them about potential involvement. You may want to consider attending a university in the city in which you eventually want to live and work so that you can gain experience and contacts at local organizations as you attend classes.

Whenever possible, network with previous graduates of programs you are considering and interview the faculty in person or at the very least via phone or email. Often, these interactions can provide you with information to aid in your application and final choice. One professor I interviewed when I was applying to graduate school actually told me that most of the students in his program were "bored housewives." Not only was his comment demeaning to his students, and let's face it, to housewives, too, but it also made clear to me that he didn't view the program as a professional stepping stone, which was what I was seeking at the time to advance me into a curatorial career.

To help navigate the variety of choices for graduate programs, I've divided the more common types of graduate degrees for museum employees into three groups: those that are discipline specific (e.g., art, history, or science); those that are museum or function specific (e.g., museum studies or conservation); and other degrees applicable to museum work such education and business.

DISCIPLINE-SPECIFIC GRADUATE DEGREES

Museum positions tied directly to creating scholarly content—curatorial or other research-related jobs—require at least a master's degree if not a doctorate in the subject area of the museum's focus, such as Baroque art, Civil War history, marine biology, etc. Subject-specific graduate degrees are also applicable to any position that involves working with objects in the collection, exhibitions, editing and writing, and education. Because professors and students in these types of graduate programs tend to be more focused on research, publication, and teaching at the university level as opposed to careers in museums, you may need to take the initiative to find museum opportunities yourself.

Some universities offer **certificates** in museum studies as an optional part of a master's or doctoral program in the humanities, especially in art history, anthropology, and history. To acquire the certificates, students take either additional courses in museum topics or choose these topics for their electives. An internship may be included in the coursework. These certificates, although not nearly as comprehensive as a master's degree in museum studies, do provide students with a useful foundation of theory and practice to prepare them for museum work.

Museum professionals who acquire subject-specific master's degrees are often faced with the choice of continuing school to obtain a doctorate, postponing the doctorate for later in life, or deciding that the master's will suffice for their career aspirations. To rise to senior-level curatorial positions a Ph.D. is mandatory, although the field of contemporary art can be more lenient for candidates with exceptional experience. Among museum directors, doctorates are fairly common but not always required depending on the museum and the director's responsibilities. A master's degree in the museum's discipline, or in museum studies, education, or business, combined with management experience may be enough to make the candidate attractive for a director's position.

Heather Ferrell, director of the Salina Art Center in Kansas, followed her undergraduate degrees (a B.A. and B.F.A.) with a master's in art history and museum studies at Case Western Reserve University. "I was invited to come back as a Ph.D. candidate in Art History at Case Western," she says,

> and I considered it, but decided to pursue a job opportunity right out of school at a museum in Fargo, North Dakota. I thought I could always return in a year or two for my Ph.D. and decide on a more specific path of study. Before I applied for the Salina Art Center position I did consider returning for my Ph.D. and talked with several colleagues—both directors and art historians. I could do the Ph.D., and I often miss the research and scholarship, however, the field doesn't suit my passions for bringing artists, community, and contemporary art together as well as serving as a director. I may still go back in a few years for a Ph.D. in art administration, or art history—but I want to explore my director position first.

Some museum curators and researchers also work at universities where they have the resources to conduct and publish primary research. While in charge of the Hayden Planetarium at the American Museum of Natural History, Neil deGrasse Tyson also taught in the Department of Astrophysical Sciences at Princeton University. He says,

> I am an academic, with roots in universities. I was called upon by the American Museum of Natural History to advise them on their need to renovate the Hayden Planetarium. So I viewed myself as a servant of the interests of the institution. But only when they agreed to establish a research department of astrophysics did I agree to leave Princeton and become director of the planetarium. My interest in working at the museum flowed directly from the creation of an academic environment. Something not all museums have the luxury of doing.

FUNCTION-SPECIFIC GRADUATE DEGREES

Degrees such as museum studies or historic preservation prepare students for careers specifically in museums or similar organizations.

Most of these programs combine an academic approach with practical training, such as internships or other hands-on opportunities. The majority of these programs offer terminal master's degrees, although a few provide doctorates, such as in public history. As mentioned with undergraduate degrees, a listing of museum studies and related graduate programs can be found on the Smithsonian's website for professional development.

In addition to offering core classes in museum management, history, theory, operations, and technology, **museum studies** programs allow students to focus on specific functions such as collections management, education, exhibitions, and administration as well as on subjects related to museum missions, such as art, anthropology, natural history, etc. Graduates from these programs obtain both knowledge and experience of best practices within the museum field and are primed to assume a variety of museum positions. The International Council of Museums has published on its website curricula guidelines for museum professional development, which is helpful to see what core competencies are expected of museum workers and their educational programs. Also see a survey by the Committee on Museum Professional Training posted on its website that gathered expectations of skills and knowledge for entry-level employees.

Lauren Telchin Katz, planning specialist in the Office of the Director of the National Museum of American History, found that her master's in museum studies from George Washington University prepared her for her current position, which combines administrative responsibilities with project management. In terms of beginning her museum career, Telchin Katz said,

> I absolutely love museums but was unsure of how to work in the field. Although my primary interest involved exploring the business of working in and running a museum, I also love museum objects. I felt that a master's degree in museum studies (after a B.A. in art history) would afford me the best opportunity to pursue a career that gives me the ability to interact with real objects, as well as work with diverse people with expertise in their subject areas.

In addition to George Washington University, some preeminent museum studies programs include

- COOPERSTOWN GRADUATE PROGRAM, NEW YORK, ADMINIS-
  TERED BY THE STATE UNIVERSITY OF NEW YORK, ONEONTA
- UNIVERSITY OF DENVER
- INDIANA UNIVERSITY-PURDUE UNIVERSITY, INDIANAPOLIS
- JOHN F. KENNEDY UNIVERSITY, BERKELEY, CALIFORNIA
- JOHNS HOPKINS UNIVERSITY, BALTIMORE
- NEW YORK UNIVERSITY, NEW YORK
- TEXAS TECH UNIVERSITY, LUBBOCK
- UNIVERSITY OF WASHINGTON, SEATTLE

Although this book is focused on U.S. institutions, no discussion of museum studies is complete without mentioning the University of Leicester, England, which is a leader in the field. It offers certificates, master's degrees, and a doctorate in museum studies, which, as of this writing, is not available at any university in the United States. Some of Leicester's programs, including the Ph.D., are available via distance learning.

As you consider which school will be right for you, determine if the program has a strength in one or two disciplines. If this isn't obvious by the program's description, look at the course listings and find out where the Museum Studies Department is located within the university's organization. For example, the University of Denver offers graduate degrees with a concentration in museum studies via their anthropology and art history departments. The master's degree from Johns Hopkins emphasizes technology and innovative practices and can be completed in part through online classes.

When researching museum studies degrees, review their professional development opportunities, including internships and fellowships, and see who is teaching the classes. Often, staff employed at museums teach classes as adjuncts in these programs. The interaction you have with these professors is priceless in terms of networking and mentoring. The same is true of networking with your classmates. Many students in museum studies programs are already working in museums or have such experience and they are acquiring the degree to enhance their knowledge, skills, and ultimately their careers. These people will be the first to know when positions open up at their own institutions and can share that information with you as well as provide you with "insider" tips on how to successfully apply and secure jobs at these museums.

Also review thesis topics and class projects, which are often posted online, to see if they appeal to you and if they are challenging enough for your aspirations. For example, if you are interested in a career with a public dimension, you may not want to apply to a program that is rich in collections management and conservation and weak in audience development and opportunities for community-based collaborations. However, do try to sample different aspects of museum work while in school to enrich your career possibilities and general knowledge. After all, effective museum educators respect and appreciate the value of object care; development officers with an appreciation for community engagement write the best grants; and curators with fundraising experience are unstoppable!

Students of **arts administration** or **arts management** programs study core managerial and leadership competencies that are translatable to cultural institutions of all variety, including visual and performing arts. These programs, although not museum-centric, prepare future arts administrators with classes on topics such as marketing and audience development, fundraising, financial management for nonprofits, governance, and community relations. For a listing of graduate and some undergraduate programs, see the website for the Association of Arts Administration Educators (AAAE). AAAE also has a searchable database of master's theses and management projects, so you can see what topics students are researching at which universities. Some of the recent museum-focused studies analyzed museum membership programs, looked at admission prices and their effect on attendance, examined the ethics of corporate sponsorship, and considered projected profit and loss trends for gift and bookstores.

A graduate degree in **public history** is becoming more common among content-producing positions such as curator, educator, and researcher, as well as collections management and administration at history-based institutions. New York University's graduate program defines public history as "history that is seen, heard, read, and interpreted by a popular audience." Essentially, public historians study history to educate humanity at large as opposed to students in formal classroom environments. In these graduate programs, students learn about such topics as historic administration, preservation practices, and community history as well as participate in internships. Eastern Illinois offers a degree specifically in historical administration to prepare their graduates to work at history museums and agencies. The online Public History Resource Center and the website for the National Council on Public History provide links to graduate schools as well as job resources.

Students of **historic preservation** learn the theory and practice of restoring, maintaining, and protecting manmade structures of historic significance. Examples of these structures include everything from a slave dwelling from the early 1800s to a 1950s skyscraper to the entire French Quarter in New Orleans. In addition to participating in internships, students in these programs take classes on topics such as preservation law and economics, conservation science, building assessment strategies, and preservation history and theory. PreservationDirectory.com and the Public History Resource Center provide listings and links to graduate programs in historic preservation, in addition to jobs, professional organizations, and events and conferences.

Museum education programs, such as those offered at the Bank Street College of Education in New York and George Washington University in DC, are tailored for students who want to learn about the fundamentals of human development as a means for creating stimulating programming and educational strategies in museums. Some museum education degrees include teacher certification and student teaching in schools as well as internships in museum education and outreach departments. This degree is applicable not just for museum education positions but any type of job that involves communicating with the public, such as exhibition developer and, of course, museum director.

In 2004, the College Art Association published on their website, guidelines for **curatorial studies** programs, which are increasingly being offered as a certificate or master's degree through art history departments. At the forefront is the Center for Curatorial Studies at Bard College in New York, which combines theoretical study with practical experience focused on contemporary art. These programs give students the opportunity to curate their own shows, work with art and artists firsthand, and network with museum professionals.

For information on more specialized degrees such as **archival**

studies, **conservation**, **informatics/information systems**, and **library studies**, see related job descriptions in Part Two.

OTHER GRADUATE DEGREES

Many museum directors, especially those running children's museums or institutions with high numbers of young audiences, possess doctorates in **education**. And it is not uncommon to find education departments staffed by former grade school or high school teachers who contribute both their experience and scholarly background. After teaching high school biology for several years, Chuck Howarth, former director and CEO of Liberty Science Center, decided to change careers. "So I did some networking to see what other kinds of employment were available for someone with my background and stumbled onto a position at the Museum of Science in Boston as a staff educator. Up to that point, I didn't even know museums had educators."

Most of the museum jobs requiring advanced **business** degrees are at mid- to large-sized institutions that have complex financial structures or marketing activities, with administrative positions such as chief operating officer, chief financial officer, deputy director, head of administrative functions, etc. Museums such as the San Francisco Museum of Modern Art or the Milwaukee Public Museum have sophisticated operations involving retail sales, food service, visitor and event ticketing, and comprehensive marketing. As of this writing, there is no M.B.A. program specifically for museums, but there are several focused on arts administration, such the University of Wisconsin, Madison, or on non-profit organizations, such as the Kellogg School of Management at Northwestern University, Evanston, Illinois.

WHICH GRADUATE PROGRAM SHOULD YOU CHOOSE?

To be honest, any of the graduate degrees mentioned above will serve you well for a museum career; you need to decide where your interests lie. Obtaining a discipline-specific degree provides you with a depth of knowledge translatable to many positions, but you may find yourself lacking in the practical skills and professional contacts gained through function-specific degree programs like museum studies. Similarly, function-specific degrees provide their graduates a jumpstart on their careers in almost any type of institution, but the generalist approach may not appeal to employers seeking applicants with more scholarly backgrounds, particularly for senior-level content-producing jobs, such as curator or educator.

Some other factors you may want to consider include:

- Tuition and expenses. Speaking from personal experience, paying back student loans stinks. If a school throws money at you, grab it!

- Location. If you're like me and you hate to move, choose a school in a city where you want to work. I chose to attend George Washington University in DC, in large part because I knew the city had thousands of museum jobs. As I completed my master's thesis in art history, I landed a job at the Smithsonian Institution, where I worked for five years.

- Study what you love. The classes will be hard and the financial costs will be high. Don't waste years of your life and thousands of dollars being miserable in hopes of gaining a great job afterward. If you'll be kicking and screaming during the entire M.B.A. program, don't sign up.

CHAPTER EIGHT
INTERNSHIPS AND VOLUNTEERING

"It is crucial that at your earliest opportunity—mine was at age twenty—get experience: volunteer, intern, contract for various duties," says Heather Ferrell, director of the Salina Art Center in Kansas. She continues:

> By the time I enrolled in graduate school I had three years museum experience in collections management, curatorial/administration, education, and special projects. I had also volunteered as a gallery director for my university and oversaw several juried art competitions. This experience really fed my desire to pursue a museum path—both curatorial and directorial—and gave me a distinct advantage.

Ferrell's words echo the recommendations of many within the museum field: gain experience as soon as possible. One of the easiest ways to accomplish this is to intern or volunteer for organizations in your community. Note that Ferrell did both. Volunteering on weekends at the local art space while interning at the science museum's Education Department doubles your professional contacts, provides you with a range of skills and practice, and demonstrates your commitment to the field when you list both on your résumé.

INTERNSHIPS

An internship is a formalized period of supervised training. Internships can be great opportunities to gain experience while in school or soon after graduation, or even for someone switching careers. Depending on the program, they can be part time or full time, highly planned with mini-courses on museum functions, or completely unstructured.

Internships are intended to provide hands-on knowledge and skills unavailable in the classroom yet necessary for a career in museum work.

An intern in a museum's Education Department might develop exhibition tours for school groups or help create teachers' resource kits. A communications intern might be tasked with researching a specific demographic, such as high school students, to better promote the museum's programs to that target audience. In the Collections Department, interns assist with cataloging and researching objects, assessing their condition, and recommending storage or conservation needs.

Internships may be project dependent as opposed to being offered regularly. For example, a curator working on a large exhibition catalog might need an intern one summer to fact-check the manuscript before going to press or to research rights and permissions for images.

Some internships provide course credit, a stipend, or nothing but prestige and a notch on your career path. The most competitive ones are those offering compensation. But participating in an internship—for credit or for free—while enrolled in school moves you one step closer to employment upon graduation.

Before going further, however, I want to stress that internships are NOT mandatory. Museum work is not like the medical field, where doctors serve as residents and gain years of experience before practicing on their own. Museum internships can be extremely helpful in gaining a foothold in the industry and they are quite common, but many people start their museum careers in other ways. If you find opportunities for paid museum employment as well as internships, consider both options. While I was in graduate school, I quit an eight-month internship after only four months because I found a full-time paying position at a different museum. When I was giving notice to my supervisor, I worried she would be unhappy at my early exit, but she actually told me I'd made a smart move and that she was proud of me.

FINDING AND APPLYING FOR MUSEUM INTERNSHIPS

If you are in high school or college, check with your career development center for any relevant contacts or information. Even if they can't offer you specific opportunities, let them know your interests. An alumna of the university where I work wanted to offer an externship to a student interested in the business of nonprofits. She called the career development center, which, after not being able to find an interested student, called us in the museum because it turned out the alumna worked for The Metropolitan Museum of Art. We had a talented student already working for us who was majoring in business who grabbed the opportunity to shadow this alumna. A year later, our student graduated and landed a job at the Met, thanks in part to the connection she made.

If your school has a museum, ask their staff about internship opportunities. To be honest, you should already be working for the university's museum anyway. They might also have specific internship or fellowship programs available to students for class credit or know about opportunities at other institutions. Staff at local museums often ask me to suggest a student or two to apply for their internships. We've even had a law firm with an art collection call us to recommend a student to catalog their artwork.

Some museums post internship opportunities on their website. You can usually find these listings in the "About" page for the museum, under "staff" or "employment," or on the Education Department's pages. But if you don't see any, don't assume none are available. Call or email the museum directly to find out.

Look for internship listings on museum listserves, employment websites, and websites for professional development. Many of these online sources are the same ones that you'll use later to find a full-time job, so the more familiar you are with them the better. Some of the more encompassing online sources include (see Appendix Three for web addresses):

- AMERICAN ASSOCIATION OF MUSEUMS' JOB CENTER
- GLOBAL MUSEUM
- MUSEUM EMPLOYMENT RESOURCE CENTER
- MUSEUMJOBS.COM
- MUSEUM-L (LISTSERVE FOR MUSEUM PROFESSIONALS)
- UNIVERSITY OF LEICESTER, DEPARTMENT OF MUSEUM STUDIES

As with job openings, internships posted on these sources are highly competitive. To improve your chances, have an advisor or supervisor assist you with the application or at least review your materials. Ask if that person knows anyone at the institution where you are applying who could put in a good word for you. And apply for more than one internship to better your chances.

If you are called in for an interview, treat the experience as if you were interviewing for a job. Show up on time, if not a little early. Dress professionally. Do your homework before the interview by learning as much as you can about the institution and why you are the ideal candidate. (See interview tips in the next chapter.) Follow up the interview with a thank-you letter or email.

Most importantly, when looking for internships, keep yourself open to all options, because internships can be a great way to find out what interests you in museums—or not. You might think that teaching children about bugs and flowers at a nature center sounds like the ideal job until you actually do it. Afterward, you'll realize that your temperament may be better suited to a position with less involvement with the public and more research. Or you might have had your heart set on an internship with a prominent curator of archeology but were assigned to the Product Development Department, only to discover that marketing is one of the most creative and vibrant activities at the museum. In either case, you will still have made inroads into the profession and gained contacts.

MAKE THE MOST OF YOUR INTERNSHIP

While you are interning, seek out opportunities to learn more about the museum and its staff. Ask your supervisor if you can be an observer or take notes in project meetings. Take your supervisor to lunch to find out more about her career path, ask her for advice, and thank her for giving you this opportunity. See if you can conduct informational interviews with her peers. Volunteer to complete any sort of "busy" work she might have piled up, such as putting away files and paperwork or adding names and addresses to mailing lists. On the other hand, if you find that your internship comprises solely of busy work, talk to your supervisor about taking on more challenging projects. But don't be discouraged, you'll be hard pressed to find a museum professional who doesn't have envelope-stuffing experience!

In the ideal scenario, an internship will lead into a full-time paid position in the same museum. But usually, the number of interns far outweighs the number of available jobs, so talk to your supervisors and fellow interns about additional opportunities for employment as well as sources for listings. And before leaving, be sure to ask your supervisor if she will be a reference for you in the future. When I look at candidates applying for entry-level jobs at our museum, the first reference I'm going to call is a museum employee, not a professor.

Most importantly, befriend your fellow interns. Yes, you might find yourself in competition for the same jobs but they are your peers. You'll quickly learn how small the museum world truly is.

VOLUNTEERING

Potential employers tend to view internships as more valuable than volunteering, in terms of professional experience, if only because the former is more structured than the latter. However, in the right circumstances, volunteering can be just as enriching and educational as an internship. For example, months of Sunday afternoons spent volunteering in the insect zoo at a science center will be more applicable to a future job in the Education Department at a children's museum than a formal internship at a prestigious institution where your major project was reorganizing the departmental files. Small museums in particular provide challenging volunteer assignments because they rely so heavily on their volunteers to assist with museum operations.

Volunteering provides more flexibility than an internship, especially if you are working full time in another position. Volunteer assignments may require just a few hours a week or a month, and many opportunities are available during the evenings for special events or on weekends. Unfortunately, this flexibility means you won't be in contact with much of the staff who work during standard office hours. But you can still network with your supervisors and fellow volunteers. When I once volunteered as a security guard at an exhibition opening, I met the organization's assistant director and learned that most of their exhibitions were proposed by independent curators. We talked about what types of exhibitions the organization was looking for and she encouraged me to submit a proposal, which ultimately led to my first curated show.

A **docent** is a volunteer who acts as a tour guide for museum visitors. Managed by the education office, docents receive regular training to maintain and gain knowledge about the museum's collections, exhibitions, and programs, as well as to learn how to develop interactive tours or activities for visitors. At some very large and prestigious organizations, the docent program is competitive, and docents may number in the hundreds. In the past, "ladies of leisure" filled the docent ranks, linking their charitable activities with their social life. Museums today seek docents with educational backgrounds or interests that can contribute to the museum's vivacity and encourage diversity.

Because not all museums post volunteer information on their websites, call the organization during regular working hours to learn about their needs and if you might qualify. Most volunteer activities are supervised or at least funneled through the Education Department. If you don't like the available volunteer assignments, ask if you can contact another department directly. Some people find that supervising interns is too demanding, but having a spare set of hands available for one or two afternoons a week is much more manageable, particularly with projects such as researching media contacts, assembling invitations for gala events, or assisting an educator with a tour.

The same advice for maximizing your internship applies to volunteer work. Talk to as many people as you can and ask them about their jobs and their experiences. Anyone you meet, including a fellow volunteer, is a contact who might lead to more opportunities. If you are great at your post, they might even hire you to supervise the volunteers.

In addition to volunteering for museums, consider volunteering for **other cultural organizations** and, if possible, **professional museum associations**. Often, key donors and "players" in the cultural landscape of a town participate not just with a museum but also with the theater, ballet, opera, etc. So working with these other organizations provides inroads into the museums through alternate avenues. Museum associations, such as the Western Museums Association or AAM, need volunteers not just to assist in their offices but especially to help with conferences and other events. Volunteering for a museum conference offers direct contact with people in the industry and will expose you not just to museums but to businesses that serve the field, such as crating and shipping companies, publishers, design and production firms, and software companies. You'll also have first crack at the posted job listings, and most organizations provide free admission to the conference in exchange for your time and hard work.

ONE FINAL NOTE

If you cannot work, intern, study, or volunteer with a museum, try gaining experience in an administrative, research, service-oriented, or nonprofit environment where you will be able to prove your potential as a vital employee. When I see that a student applying for one of our jobs worked every summer as a server at the same restaurant, I know that she is a reliable hard worker who will contribute to our program, even if she has little museum experience.

CHAPTER NINE

FINDING AND APPLYING FOR JOBS

Let's face it—landing that ideal museum post is a challenge, to say the least. The museum field is extremely competitive, especially in larger metropolitan areas with several prestigious museums. The following suggestions are intended to help you maximize your ability to find job openings and apply as a strong candidate, with error-free résumés, confident interviews, and appropriate follow-up. At the end of the chapter are ideas on what to do when you are doing everything "right" yet a museum job remains elusive.

FINDING JOB OPENINGS

There are several avenues for locating available museum positions; try them ALL, because there's no single complete source for museum job openings. Below are several different approaches. See Appendix Three for website addresses.

1. **Look up jobs on websites dedicated to the museum industry**. These include the following:

- AMERICAN ASSOCIATION OF MUSEUMS JOB CENTER
- GLOBAL MUSEUM
- MUSEUM EMPLOYMENT RESOURCE CENTER
- MUSEUMJOBS.COM
- MUSEUM-L (LISTSERVE FOR MUSEUM PROFESSIONALS)
- UNIVERSITY OF LEICESTER, DEPARTMENT OF MUSEUM STUDIES

These websites feature jobs throughout the country and abroad that are highly competitive and quite varied. Also look for listings on regional museum association websites such as the New England Museum Association or the California Association of Museums.

If you're uncertain as to what type of museum work you'd like to pursue, read the many listings on these sites to see what is available and what they require. But remember, these sites also tend to post more upper- and mid-level positions as opposed to entry-level ones (e.g., directors and senior managers vs. assistant type jobs).

2. **Research listings on subject-specific or profession-specific association websites.** If you know you want to work at a history museum or as an art educator, determine the professional associations for those types of employees and check their websites for job listings, such as the AASLH or the Natural Sciences Collections Alliance. For profession-specific organizations, read the job descriptions in Part Two, where you'll learn about listings in the *Chronicle of Philanthropy* for fundraising jobs or the Visual Resources Association for information management positions.

3. **Look up jobs on websites dedicated to nonprofit careers.** These websites seem to be increasing rapidly in number. They may have positions not included in more museum-focused sites—positions such as an operations manager or product branding assistant. You'll also find listings for associations or organizations that have positions with responsibilities translatable to museum work. Some of the more popular websites for nonprofit employment include:

- IDEALIST.ORG
- NONPROFITOYSTER.COM
- NONPROFIT.CAREERBUILDER.COM
- NONPROFITCAREERS.ORG

4. **Research museum jobs in general employment sources.** These include local newspaper classifieds and websites such as Craig's list and Indeed.com—I've seen listings from museum director to cashier on these jobs sites. In general, entry-level positions, such as administrative assistant, gallery attendant, and development assistant or seasonal and part-time positions, are easy enough to fill with local applicants, so museums advertise locally.

5. **Contact museums directly.** Many museums post available positions on their websites. You can often find links to job listings via their "about" or "info" link on their main website, or just run a search for "employment" on their site. You can always call a museum directly

and ask if they have any openings. They may not bother posting entry-level, seasonal, and part-time position openings on their website, so you'll never hear about these jobs otherwise. I landed my first full-time museum job by calling the museum directly and applying for the position before they had even advertised the job.

6. **Network.** If you are interning, volunteering, working part time, or involved in any capacity with a museum, tell your supervisor and peers that you are looking for a job and ask if they have heard of any openings. If you interned for a museum in the past, contact your previous supervisor and ask him or her if he or she knows of any available jobs. Attend events at museums and association conferences so you can meet more museum professionals who might know of current or upcoming opportunities. Everyone in the industry is aware of the difficulties of the job search. If you show you're a hard worker who is efficient and creative, you'll find people willing to help you at different stages of your career.

APPLYING FOR MUSEUM JOBS
RÉSUMÉS, APPLICATIONS, AND COVER LETTERS

A clean, well-organized, typo-free **résumé** containing basic and relevant work and educational experience is appropriate when applying for most entry- to mid-level positions. Résumé templates abound on the Internet as well in several word-processing software programs.

If possible, ask a museum employee in your field of interest to review your résumé because the standard professional format is fine for many but not all museum jobs. For example, instead of a résumé, a museum curator has a curriculum vitae (CV), which is a document that lists every relevant professional position, exhibition, catalog, book, published article, professional affiliation, and conference presentation achieved by the applicant. For guidelines on drafting a CV, see the College Art Association's website. That's far too much information for someone applying for an entry-level position, but don't be afraid to go beyond one page if your experience and education warrant more space.

A supervisor or mentor can also help you identify responsibilities, tasks, promotions, and awards that you accomplished in prior positions that are valuable in the job market. Think of ways to amplify your professional experience to be relevant to museum positions. Here are some examples:

GALLERY ATTENDANT
(UNIVERSITY MUSEUM, PART-TIME, 2007–2009)

Responsibilities included greeting all museum visitors and being knowledgeable about museum and university facilities and programs; overseeing visitor activities within the galleries to maintain a safe and secure environment; assisting the curator of education with developing and giving exhibition tours for freshmen in a general-education class; proofreading the museum's press releases, brochures, and other printed items; and assisting with assembling materials for mass-mailing fundraising campaigns.

RETAIL MANAGER
(HOUSEWARES STORE, 2007–2009)

Responsibilities included supervising ten full-time and part-time workers as well as establishing work schedules, facilitating payroll, and overseeing customer relations initiatives; implementing new merchandise and window displays; and assisting with developing local advertising campaigns.

RECEPTIONIST
(MCQUEEN & SMITH INSURANCE COMPANY, 2007–2009)

Responsibilities included answering phones and greeting customers, updating the office's website, handling all mailing services, writing and distributing meeting notes, maintaining the office files, ordering supplies, and proofreading brochures and printed matter.

With the last two examples, the responsibilities, although not directly related to museum work, reveal your professionalism, organizational abilities, and creativity as well as experience working with the public—all very important qualities for a museum employee. If you can't think of any way to connect your work experience to museum responsibilities—a yearlong stint as a professional dog walker, for example—still consider listing those jobs and your tenure because potential employers need to know that you are a reliable hard worker. The last thing an employer wants to do is teach someone "how" to work, meaning how important it is to show up on time, follow through on assignments, respect coworkers and supervisors, etc.

Do include special skills that may be appropriate. Examples include fluency in foreign languages, experience with making frames or cabinetry, or familiarity with collections management, fundraising, financial, or graphic design software. As you accrue more experience, you can begin creating a portfolio of materials that demonstrate your accomplishments, such as copies of published articles, brochures that you wrote and designed, samples of successful fundraising materials, and even annual reports.

You can list names and contact information of professional **references** on your résumé or you can write "references available upon request." The latter option gives you the chance to connect with your references in advance of the organization, so you can give them information about the job for which you're applying and what types of things you'd like them to mention. Be sure to have three references available at any time and include at least one person who was your direct supervisor. Only list your current supervisor as a reference if you are certain that doing so will not jeopardize your working relationship.

Unless you are absolutely sure your potential employer shares your opinions and sensibilities, do not include on your résumé or application any membership or volunteer activities with political parties, religious organizations, or any other sort of association that engenders polarized responses. Obviously, if you have relevant work experience with any of these types of organizations include your job under "professional experience" and describe your duties and accomplishments. But otherwise, do not give out information about yourself that could be negatively viewed by the person reading your application.

Museums with parent organizations, especially those that belong to government agencies, may require **application forms**, which will be posted on the website of the museum or its parent institution. Much of the information required in the application duplicates that of the résumé, in addition to items such as your nationality, previous or current employment status at the parent organization, racial and gender identity, and any special eligibility status you may have such as being a veteran of the armed services. You may be able to apply for these positions online, but remember to proof any material before submission. And if you know someone already working at the parent organization or familiar with the submission process, ask that person to review your application for tips on content and format.

Look closely at the job description to address necessary experience and skills that will help the people reviewing applications determine the strongest candidates. This is especially important for jobs at a museum with a parent organization or at an extremely large institution. The U.S. government calls these qualities "ranking factors," and examples include "experience with collections development and donor cultivation," "knowledge of federal procurement procedures," "skill in developing communications plans," and "experience with automated systems."

These factors can be included in the "experience" section in your résumé or application, or can be discussed in your **cover letter**. I don't know if anyone has studied how potential employers review incoming applications, but in my office we look at the résumé first, then the cover letter, which should be articulate and informative. A poorly written cover letter with typos or mistakes jeopardizes a candidate's chance. Do not repeat information in the letter that is obvious from your résumé. Instead, discuss those factors mentioned above to prove that you are clearly suited for the position and how your strengths compliment those of the institution, its mission, and its goals. The cover letter is also the proper place to do the following:

- name drop: "I enjoyed working with Jane Smith, current president of the museum's board, at a recent volunteer book drive at the local library. Ms. Smith discussed with me the many exciting educational programs planned for the museum in the upcoming year."

- expound on items in your résumé: "I became familiar with the museum's collection of glassware when I met the staff in the Decorative Arts Department this past spring to research my master's thesis on drinking vessels from the 19th century. Claire Johnson, curatorial assistant, in particular assisted me in reviewing the accession records of the extensive Danbury collection of glassware."

- highlight your accomplishments: "One of my accomplishments as development assistant at the McSmith Art Museum was working with a board member to reorganize and re-energize the Collectors Circle. Over a two-year period we increased this group's membership from 20 to 200, which resulted in the donation of funds to buy two major contemporary photographs for the permanent collection, in addition to unrestricted funds that were used to assist children's programs."

- explain why you are looking for a new job: "My current position as public affairs assistant has prepared me with essential PR experience and media contacts that I can now use to create a communications plan for larger projects and institutions."

Proof read your letter, résumé, and application before submission. Show them to a peer, supervisor, friend, relative, or anyone you know who will be able to catch typos and ask you about phrases that are unclear or confusing.

After you submit your application, try to be patient waiting for a response. Museums can be notoriously slow in hiring people, and the larger the institution often the longer the process. If, after a few weeks, you haven't received notification from the museum, contact the recipient to confirm they received your application.

The Job Interview

Typically, museums invite viable local candidates for in-person interviews. Mid- to upper-level position candidates from further away are usually interviewed over the phone first by their potential supervisor who then decides if they should be invited to visit the museum. When scheduling your interview, **ask the museum representative to identify the person(s) you will be meeting**. In addition to your potential supervisor, you might also meet with someone in the Human Resources Department or the museum manager, as well as potential coworkers or other higher-ups within the institution such as the director or a board member. The more senior the open position, the more people you will meet. And Curatorial Department interviews often consist of a panel review during which the candidate is grilled on her or his experience, opinions, research, and knowledge of her or his field.

Prior to the interview, **research** as much as you can about the museum, the people you will be meeting, and the department to which you are applying. If you live nearby, visit the museum once or twice before your meeting. Showing up at an interview without ever having stepped foot in the door is inexcusable unless you live far away. Also, read everything relevant on the museum's website, look up their catalogs and any other publications by the museum available in their gift store and at your local library, and ask anyone you know who works in museums for advice. A student once called me the day before a job interview only to learn that I had actually applied and interviewed for that very same position ten years ago. I was able to give her a few tips, and she landed the job.

While you are conducting your research, **assemble a set of questions or ideas** that you can discuss during the interview. At some point the interviewer will ask, "Do you have any questions?" and the last thing you want to say is, "no" because it demonstrates a lack of interest. Examples of questions appropriate to different positions include, "How many catalogs does the museum publish per year?" "What is your advertising budget?" "What sort of interface do staff members have with the board?" "What type of collections software do you use?" "What school groups are targeted with educational programs?" You may not have time to ask all of your prepared questions but you want to prove your competence and knowledge of the field, your curiosity about the position and the museum, and your ability to converse with your peers.

You can also ask questions about the job itself, with topics such as the average number of weekly hours, anticipated overtime, benefits, opportunities for professional development, the department's and the museum's organizational structure, who your supervisor's supervisor would be, how projects are assigned, and how feedback is provided. Always ask about their decision-making process for choosing the final candidate and how long they anticipate the job search to last.

A few museums post **salary** information with the job description but many do not. And some may ask for your salary history. If the salary is not included in the listing, I advise asking about it at the end of your meeting with the supervisor or with the human resources representative, if you meet with one. If you are asked, "What is your current salary?" do not feel that you have to answer that question. After all, you might be currently working in a woefully underpaid museum job, which is the reason you're looking for a new position, or you might be making a healthy salary in the private sector but you're ready to sacrifice some income to enter the museum industry. You can respond with "I'm seeking a position that pays in the range of $35,000 to $40,000 [or whatever range you are seeking]." Generally, if any negotiating occurs it will be after the first interview, when you've been contacted for a second interview or offered the position. Whatever you do, don't increase the figure once you've chosen one and be prepared to walk away if you truly need more than they are offering.

In terms of **attire**, a suit is always appropriate for a job interview, particularly with the more formal museum departments such as development, finance, or the director's office. **Prior to and during the interview...**

- Allow yourself enough time to find the museum, locate a parking space, or walk from the bus stop and arrive at the office a few minutes early.

- Bring a copy of your résumé or application, cover letter, and any other relevant items such as writing samples in addition to your list of questions and a pen or pencil.

- Ask for a business card or write down the name and title of every person you meet.

- If appropriate, take notes during the interview. By which I mean don't write down everything being said but things that you want to recall later such as upcoming project ideas.

- Never complain or speak poorly about your previous jobs, coworkers, or supervisors. This makes you appear to be unprofessional and bitter.

- Don't arrive hungry—eat a snack before the interview. Yes, I know I sound like your mother, but I once had an interview that lasted almost five hours and was never offered anything to eat or drink. I was starving and very cranky by the end of that interview!

Follow Up

Within a week after your interview **write a letter or email** to everyone you met who spent a significant amount of time with you, meaning twenty minutes or more. This could include the human resources manager who discussed the museum's benefits, the potential coworker who showed you around the office and collections storage areas, and the supervisor for the position. If you met with a committee, address the point person for the group, who was probably your potential supervisor anyway.

To all but your primary interviewer, these can be brief, typed notes. Do not send handwritten notes or cards as they appear unprofessional. Here is a sample email that could be sent to someone in the personnel office:

Dear Mr. Johnson,

Thank you for meeting with me on Tuesday the 18th to discuss the museum's hiring policies and benefits package. I especially appreciate you taking the time to review health insurance options for families and the institution's Flex plans.

After meeting staff from many departments, it became clear to me that the museum is an institution that encourages the employees' personal and professional development. I certainly hope to enjoy these opportunities in the future as Public Relations Assistant in the museum's Communications Department.

Sincerely,
Alice Jones
105 Main Street
Houston, TX 77004
ajones@yahoo.com

[always include your contact information in these emails to remind the recipient who you are and which position you've applied for]

Here is a sample email that could be sent to a potential coworker:

Dear Ms. Folsom,

Thank you for meeting with me on Tuesday, January 18th, to discuss the responsibilities of the Public Relations Assistant and to give me a tour of the Communications offices. I was incredibly impressed by both the level of activity amongst the staff and their professional and pleasant demeanor. Despite the pressure of the impending opening of the exhibition "Mummies to Pharaohs: the Myths and Magic of Egypt," every person I met was kind enough to stop, introduce themselves, and discuss their role in the upcoming events. I imagine that it must be invigorating to work in such a vibrant, creative, and collegial environment. Thank you again for your time.

Sincerely,
Alice Jones
105 ...

The letter or email to your potential supervisor should be more thorough than the others, include any information requested during the interview, and underscore your strengths.

Dear Ms. Spears,

Thank you for meeting with me on Tuesday, January 18th to discuss the position of Public Relations Assistant. I appreciate the time that you and your staff took to show me the office, introduce me to the department, and discuss the responsibilities of the position.

I was particularly excited to hear that the next large-scale campaign will promote the newly installed Japanese tea house. As I mentioned in the interview, I minored in Asian studies, and I'm currently a volunteer at the Japanese Cultural Association in town. My knowledge and contacts with local Asian media outlets and organizations could be beneficial to this particular project.

Likewise, my experience and skills that I have garnered as a part-time assistant in the PR office at the local children's museum will help with general media coverage of your museum's varied exhibitions and programs. The position of Public Relations Assistant at your museum will allow me to combine this knowledge with my enthusiasm for local history and culture.

As we discussed, I've enclosed a list of references at the end of this note. Please don't hesitate to contact me if you have any questions or need additional information.

Thank you again for your consideration.

Sincerely,
Alice Jones
105 ...

If you are invited to a **second interview**, follow the same advice as above but be prepared for more in-depth grilling by your interviewers. They will want to know why you are the best candidate for the job, why you want to work for their museum specifically, why you are looking for a new job in the first place, what ideas you can bring to the museum to change and improve things, and, as always, what questions you have. Follow up the second interview with emails or comments to anyone new that you met on this round and another note to the supervisor with specific responses to your discussions.

Then wait to hear from them. This can be excruciating, but badgering a potential employer never helps. If you haven't heard from the museum after a reasonable time period based on how long they said the job search would take, call or email the human resources contact or the primary interviewer and ask about the progress in filling the position. If a month passes and there's still no word, try again.

Remember that there may be factors affecting the position about which you are unaware. Some random examples include the supervisor becoming ill or being called for jury duty, thus being unable to finish the job search; the position was earmarked for an overqualified intern who has toiled away at the museum for years; or the position's slot was canceled by the parent organization to prevent other layoffs.

No matter what happens, even if you never hear back from the museum, do NOT send them a note criticizing their actions. As I mention often, the museum industry is small. Chances are, that nasty email you send to the staff member will be copied and forwarded to her coworkers, friends, and peers with a derisive heading, thereby blackballing you from opportunities at all of those museums in the future.

Consider an interview a minor battle victory in the war of becoming gainfully employed. Each one presents the opportunity to learn about the museum, the profession, and yourself.

WHAT TO DO WHEN IT'S NOT WORKING

Say you follow all of the tips above and despite your best efforts you still don't have a full-time job at a museum. Unfortunately, this is not an uncommon scenario. As I've said throughout this book, the museum job market is highly competitive and unlikely to change in the foreseeable future. In some cases, it's just a matter of being at the right place at the right time when a job opens up that is perfect for you. That is not helpful advice, but it is intended to be somewhat consoling in knowing that you are not in complete control of the situation. Just because you can't land a job doesn't mean you are failing your job search. It just means that opportunities are not available to you for a variety of possibly unknowable reasons. If you find yourself in this frustrating situation, it may be time to start expanding your target to look for alternatives to your ideal museum job.

Consider applying for jobs in departments other than what you'd planned. No matter the position, any museum job when you are starting your career will provide you with valuable experience and contacts and with a head start for when the position you really want opens up. For example, your dream may be to become a curator of contemporary art, but positions in that department are practically impossible to secure without a Ph.D. and a track record of exhibitions. So you apply for and receive a job in the education office as an assistant, helping run the teen advisory council that organizes special events and exhibitions for kids in high schools. The experience you gain from this position in terms of facilitating collaborations with the local community and learning how community members can impact how the museum operates and interprets its mission will serve you throughout your museum career, no matter where you end up.

If you give alternate job choices a chance, you might find that you have an affinity for different museum functions. And often you'll discover interesting positions that seem "hidden" unless you are working within the institution. These are jobs with responsibilities that are not common to every museum or are found in larger institutions, such as corporate events coordinator, exhibition evaluator, multimedia communications manager, or graphic designer for wayfinding. Just be sure not to mention your ulterior motives in your job interview because employers won't hire people who are planning to bolt as soon as the position they really want becomes available.

Apply for jobs in museums with different disciplines. Ever since you were given your first model airplane you've aspired to work with all things aviation. Yet positions at the local air and space museum rarely open up and when they do, you find yourself competing with hundreds of applicants. Start looking at job listings at all types of museums in your area. Many of the responsibilities of museum positions translate from one discipline to another. As a PR assistant at the local historical society, the media contacts and experience you acquire promoting exhibitions and events can only make you a stronger candidate when a similar position opens at the air and space museum.

Consider jobs at other arts and nonprofit institutions. All the points made above apply to this suggestion as well. That is, when you are just beginning a career, many of the skills, contacts, and experience you'll gain working for almost any type of nonprofit organization will make you a stronger candidate for museum jobs later. For example, if you end up as an assistant in the director's office of a women's service organization, you'll learn about board communications, strategic planning, project management, nonprofit fiscal management, and fundraising, to name just a few of the director's responsibilities, not to mention all the contacts you'll make with other staff members and volunteers, who may at some point become sources of information for jobs at cultural institutions as well as valuable peers and references.

Look for jobs at businesses that provide supplies or services to museums. Because so many museum functions are being outsourced to save on costs, your ideal museum job might not be in a museum. This is especially true of functions that require sophisticated skills and/or equipment, such as exhibition design and production, architecture, project management, programmatic evaluation, marketing, and information systems. The creativity and cutting-edge services that these businesses provide reinvigorate the museum field and can offer you an exciting work environment. But these firms tend to be located in larger cosmopolitan areas, where enough museums and cultural organizations exist to provide a client base. Which leads to the next suggestion ...

Consider moving. One of the drawbacks to museum work mentioned in Part One is geographic limitations—job opportunities are limited to the number of museums in your area. Once you begin considering relocating for a job, your chances of securing one increase. Obviously, you have to weigh the benefits versus costs of uprooting your life for a position that may or may not be the right fit. On the other hand, moving from institution to institution over time can propel you to the career promotions you desire. Moving to a city that hosts several museums prior to securing a new job is risky but often pays off, especially if it makes you available for entry-level positions that are not advertised widely and generally can be filled with qualified applicants in the area. But be aware that moving to a larger city means you'll be competing with yet more and possibly better-qualified applicants. When I worked in DC, there was a rumor that jobs at a very distinguished museum were so competitive that every departmental secretary had a doctorate. This meant that any time a non-administrative position opened up, the applicant pool consisted of highly educated and qualified people already employed by the institution and waiting to pounce on every opportunity.

Participate in professional development opportunities. Conferences, for-credit and noncredit classes, certificate programs, workshops, etc., all assist you in your job search as you increase your skill sets and your contacts. Professional development doesn't have to be limited to programs specifically for museum professionals. If you realize that your interests lie in producing books, catalogs, and other printed and written materials, you can attend certificate and/or noncredit classes in editing and design to learn more about those fields in general and the latest methods, theories, tools, and software available. You can learn more about professional development by contacting related associations mentioned in the job descriptions in Part Two as well as by reading Chapter Ten.

Consider Graduate School. I hesitate to recommend this because I sometimes hear former students saying, "I can't get a job so I might as well go back to school." School should not be your fallback position, if only because it's such an extremely expensive option that doesn't guarantee future employment. If, however, you find yourself being turned down for jobs repeatedly or you see your promotions being capped because you lack an advanced degree, then it might be worth the time, money, and hard work to attend graduate school. Graduate degrees can also provide you with a jumpstart into a new profession. If you have worked in museum retail and discover a passion for collections management, a museums studies program with intensive focus on objects research, care, and informatics could be your entrée into this segment of the museum world.

Be patient and adjust your expectations. I'm only including this annoying suggestion in case you are brand new to the museum world and unfamiliar with museums' slow hiring processes and the imbalanced ratio of job-seekers to job openings. One afternoon, I received a call from a former undergraduate student who assisted me in researching artwork for a modest online exhibition. Following graduation, the student landed a job in admissions at a large museum, but it was a temporary position and he needed something permanent and full time. So he contacted me for suggestions. He wanted to work with exhibitions, helping curators research and write exhibition text. I explained that those types of positions are often the most sought after in museums and that typically they require applicants to possess a master's degree if not a doctorate. Then I asked him how long he'd been looking for and applying for jobs. I heard a heavy sigh and he responded, "A whole month!" I almost hung up the phone. "A month is nothing!" I exclaimed. "Some jobs are posted for an entire month before they even begin looking at applications." "Oh," he said, "can you tell that to my dad?"

CHAPTER TEN

PROFESSIONAL DEVELOPMENT AND CAREER GROWTH

You land a job. Now what do you do?

PROFESSIONAL DEVELOPMENT

For most museum employees, the learning never stops because the knowledge and skills demanded of these museum professions constantly change. To stay on top of your field, engage in as many opportunities for professional development as possible. Examples of these types of activities include continuing your education formally with degrees or certificates or informally with noncredit classes, conferences and workshops, and relevant publications. Conferences, in particular, provide you with information on technology, research, and changes in your field and give you unlimited opportunities to meet other museum professionals.

The job descriptions in Part Two include names of professional associations such as the Museum Store Association or the Association of Fundraising Professionals that are job specific and offer all sorts of resources for continuing education. Organizations for different types of museums also offer specialized training. For example, the Association of Zoos and Aquariums provides classes on everything from crocodilian biology and management to techniques for butterfly conservation to institutional record keeping.

AAM provides continuing education and resources for all types of museums and workers and it hosts a large annual conference in late spring that attracts thousands of people from around the world. Throughout the year, it also offers workshops and subject-specific seminars, online resources, magazines, and other publications, in addition to member benefits like reduced rates on insurance and free admission to certain museums throughout the country. Regional museum associations likewise provide opportunities to meet your peers and learn more about your field. The Getty Leadership Institute manages a number of programs for senior-level museum professionals at all types of museums, and the American Association for State and Local History organizes an annual seminar for historical administration. When possible, take advantage of mid-career mentoring opportunities at museum conferences and workshops.

But don't just attend conferences, become an active participant. Organizations issue calls for participation in panel and poster sessions well in advance of their conferences. Read them over carefully and think about topics that you can speak about or report on, based on your own experience, scholarship, or observations. Better yet, organize your own session. Organizations have varying ways to decide which sessions will be included. Some, such as the College Art Association, request submissions for panel topics first and then put forth an open call for papers to all their members. AAM, on the other hand, receives session proposals with predetermined speakers and in some cases with sponsorship from subcommittees. No matter which conference I propose topics to, I am always advised to incorporate materials or approaches to enliven the panel, such as encouraging dialog from the beginning of the session rather than just having panelists read their papers and take questions afterwards. There is a tendency for some sessions to be reduced into extended "show and tells," which can be useful if the shared information is applicable to most of the audience, but after a full day of listening to papers and presentations, hearing yet another success story can become grating.

Attending these events can easily cost hundreds if not more than a thousand dollars if they are held in large and expensive cities. Being a session chair or panelist does not guarantee free admission. But volunteering usually does. So find out early on if the organization can use your services. Always ask your supervisor if the museum can pay for your membership dues or your participation and travel for workshops and conferences. If not, find out if the hosting organization offers any membership discounts and/or travel grants that you might be eligible for. Travel grants are typically limited to professionals new to museum work or those employed at museums with modest budgets for training. Remember that professional expenses not covered by your institution are tax deductible.

You can, however, continue to educate yourself by simply visiting as many museums as possible in your hometown and when you travel. When you visit museums, study how they operate and function in areas that interest you, such as how they structure and promote their membership or how they create and edit exhibition labels and panels. Attend museum lectures, guided tours, and other available programs. Introduce yourself to the staff person organizing these events and you'll learn even more.

Read relevant publications and websites, such as globalmuseum.org or the news section on the website for the International Council of Museums. Consider signing up for Museum-L, a listserve for museum professionals or for other listserves specific to your job. AAM publishes *Museum* and lists hundreds of books on their online bookstore, which you can probably borrow from your library.

Look beyond the immediate museum-focused resources to enhance your knowledge and training. Examples could include attending seminars for grade-school teachers to learn new educational approaches and theories or joining the local chamber of commerce to be introduced to your town's economic leaders and take advantage of their events focused on business enhancement. Seek out conferences that relate to your job's function but are not just for museums, such as the International Association of Amusement Parks and Attractions or the National Art Education Association. Read books and journals about education, nonprofit management, marketing trends, consumer culture, etc., practically anything that could relate to museum work.

Obviously, if you find yourself seeking a major change, such as realizing you want to be a textiles conservator after you've served a few years in the Education Department, you'll probably need to return to school for a graduate degree specific to that field. In fact, many museum professionals choose to pursue these degrees in mid-career, which can be challenging but also very rewarding as these people have definite goals in sight and have figured out how to get there. Some common degrees for early and mid-career museum professionals are museum studies, education, preservation, business, or discipline-specific degrees such as history, which may involve proceeding on to a doctorate.

CAREER GROWTH

Sure it's possible that you obtain your dream job and you live happily ever after, working in a state of bliss, waking up every morning with a sense of purpose and ending every day with a feeling of accomplishment. But if you're like me and many other people in the museum field, it can take a while before you either figure out your true calling or until you finally gain that position you've wanted from the very beginning. Certainly there are some museum professionals who have successfully maneuvered a traditional, straightforward career trajectory. And that's an effective approach, too, but it's not possible for everyone, especially as the museum industry becomes ever more lean and competitive.

I started as a receptionist at a museum, became a membership assistant, realized I wanted to be a curator so I moved to another city and went back to school for my master's degree in art history. Then I became a project director at a traveling exhibitions service and started curating exhibitions independently until I finally found a curatorial job that was available at a salary and level of responsibility that I was seeking, eleven years after I completed my undergraduate degree. I, which by this time meant "we," had to relocate for the new position, which actually has been even more rewarding than I imagined and has subsequently taken me on several different paths that I didn't expect—including writing a publication about how to get a job in a museum! When students come to me seeking career advice, I recommend being open to different opportunities because you never know what you might come across as you begin and proceed in your career.

So what is your next step? In addition to reading the position descriptions in Part Two, another way to determine if you want to rise within your field or change to another one is to read job listings at other museums. You'll quickly learn what challenges lay ahead for senior-level positions, how their responsibilities vary per museum size and type, and what kind of experience and education you'll need to succeed. You may also find that the only opportunities for promotion exist at museums in other cities.

Look closely at your own department's organization, and, if possible, network with your supervisors as much as you can to learn more about their jobs and their own career paths. Invite your supervisor to lunch, or, if you find yourself standing next to him at a museum function, strike up a conversation about how he ended up where he is today. Most people enjoy talking about themselves and offering advice, so chances are he'll be flattered to discuss his career with you.

Also speak with people in different departments. At museums with long staff tenure, it's common for employees to transfer to different jobs as they gain experience and learn more about their own work styles and interests. You'll find that some people in entry-level positions took their jobs to simply gain a foothold in the museum but have plans to move into other departments as soon as a position becomes available.

Gaining experience in other types of museum jobs allows you to confirm or change your interests and specialties and can be a means of career advancement particularly at smaller organizations. This is especially true for those seeking top-level administrative positions or directorships. D.D. Hilke, president/CEO of The Children's Museum of Utah and Discovery Gateway Project, advises learning about other museum professions through professional development. "At conferences like AAM or ASTC, instead of going to sessions in my own field, I'd attend sessions about what my colleagues did in other areas so I could respond better to my peers and also prepare myself for a directorship position."

Terri S. Rouse, CEO for Visitor Services, Capitol Visitor Center, U.S. Capitol, Washington, DC, advises ambitious museum professionals not to settle for just any available position.

> I interviewed once for a job at a big museum in New York. I had completed three advanced degrees and I was told to take whatever job I could to get my foot in a specific museum's door. But I thought why would I do that? Instead, I became a curator at the Studio Museum in Harlem. So that's what I tell young people in this field. There are museums out there that can and do pay well. They are always looking for people with excellent skills. You just need to be flexible. You need to look at your skills and convince others that you can do the job. You don't have to do "anything" to work in a museum.

Because much of the above suggestions concern maneuvering within your current institution, I'll include a brief note about **museum politics**. Every museum, no matter size, location, or discipline, has its own form of politics at play within the organization, meaning the interrelationships involving authority and influence that affect the museum's functions. Some people are well attuned to internal politics and can work the "system" to their advantage, whereas other people have a harder time assessing these types of relationships and interactions, which means they can miss out on opportunities that they aren't even aware of.

You would be wise to study how different staff members interact and successfully—or unsuccessfully—meet their objectives. Who has the director's ear? Whose opinion carries the most weight at meetings? Who is best at consensus building, and how does that person use that ability to accomplish his or her goals? I'm not suggesting you pattern yourself after that person, but observing how he or she operates and how decisions are made can assist you with your own aspirations.

As you claw your way to the corner office, always keep in mind how interconnected the museum industry truly is. People in this field love to share war stories, and the Internet has only made that easier. My career motto has always been "form no enemies," because adversaries of any type always turn into detriments on the way to happiness and success. So, although some folks consider me to be too nice, I know that keeping all doors open has benefited my professional opportunities more than once. My sphere of "niceness" also includes anyone who works for me, especially students and interns, because you just never know who might be your next boss.

LIFE OUTSIDE OF THE MUSEUM

The final tidbit of advice is to remember that life exists outside of the museum, not just the museum you work for but also the industry as a whole. Many people joke that a museum career is not a job, it's a lifestyle. We spend our free time visiting museums, learning about our field, reading the latest publications on how to create an engaging visitor experience or how to start a capital campaign from scratch. This dedication is not symptomatic of museum workers exclusively but of people working for any type of nonprofit organization who have the luxury of choosing to work in their fields. Despite the low salaries, competitive job market, and finite number of opportunities, we have the freedom to decide that we want to participate in the museum industry, and that sort of choice isn't an option for everyone on this planet.

So try to remember the world beyond your museum job and especially think about your family, friends, and community. As with any profession, the more senior level the position in a museum, the more demands are placed on the employee. It can be easy to forget the struggles and triumphs outside of your job as you become more absorbed in your work. And there is never enough time to finish everything—there never will be. When I leave the office every day, I listen to the national news on the radio, which usually gives me a quick jolt of reality before I turn my attention to my family. I also volunteer with organizations that have nothing to do with the arts or museums. Being a board member of my daughter's child care center taught me the responsibilities and pressures that such a position holds, the hard work required of board members, and the challenges facing early childhood education. It also taught me that my next volunteer stint will be as a "worker bee" and not a trustee!

But whatever you choose to do as your "other" passion—besides museums—enjoy the challenges that lay ahead of you. I was actually going to recommend becoming a well-rounded person until I read the quote below from a speech titled "The Wonderful World of Storytelling," by science fiction writer Bruce Sterling (1991).

"Don't become a well-rounded person. Well-rounded people are smooth and dull.

Become a thoroughly spiky person."

APPENDIXES

ONE
SALARIES FOR TEN COMMON POSITIONS AS SURVEYED BY REGIONAL MUSEUM ASSOCIATIONS

TWO
SALARIES FOR TEN COMMON POSITIONS AS SURVEYED BY MUSEUM PROFESSIONAL ASSOCIATIONS

THREE
ORGANIZATIONS AND WEBSITES FOR STUDENTS AND MUSEUM PROFESSIONALS

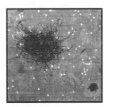

APPENDIX ONE

SALARIES FOR TEN COMMON POSITIONS
AS SURVEYED BY REGIONAL MUSEUM ASSOCIATIONS

These ten jobs were chosen to represent senior-, middle-, and entry-level positions common to different sizes of museums. These salaries were garnered from surveys by regional museum associations. See below for information on the associations.

SURVEY YEAR	AMM 2007	CAM 2006	FAM 2001
DIRECTOR (OVERALL AVERAGE)	115,809	99,750	63,668
DIRECTOR* (SMALL MUSEUM, FY$/SALARY)	<500K/51,056	<100K/35,644	<100K/30,389
DEVELOPMENT OFFICER	86,933	81,081	54,643
DEVELOPMENT/ MEMBERSHIP ASSISTANT	36,001	33,929	20,557
PUBLIC RELATIONS MANAGER	58,514	44,556	38,474
CHIEF CURATOR	56,635	49,000	62,499
CURATORIAL ASSISTANT	30,682	31,180	21,867
REGISTRAR	40,620	34,181	29,493
EDUCATION DIRECTOR	51,812	42,460	44,163
EDUCATION ASSISTANT	28,222	29,307	22,784

*Director (small museum) represents the average salary of directors in the lowest fiscal budget category in the survey.

AMM Association of Midwest Museums, *Wage & Salary Survey 2007*

CAM California Association of Museums, *2006 Survey of Museum Personnel*
Note: Because CAM's survey results are organized by budget size, an overall salary average per position is not available. The salaries above are averages from museums with annual budgets of $1 to $2.5 million.

FAM Florida Association of Museums, *Salary Survey of Museum Personnel 2001*

MANY 2006/07	NEMA 2004/2005	SEMC 2006	VAM 2005
92,398	79,003	90,700	64,295
00K to 200K/10,078	<50K/21,278	<50K/33,300	<50K/27,667
55,798	72,565	49,900	59,676
31,929	31,952	35,000	31,019
35,208	49,521	29,500	n/a
48,903	55,598	63,000	43,003
28,715	27,960	n/a	26,883
49,902	39,908	37,500	n/a
45,129	42,010	46,000	36,999
32,184	27,164	23,400	n/a

MANY Museum Association of New York, *2006—07 Salary and Benefits Survey*
Note: Because MANY's survey results are organized by budget size, an overall average salary per position is not available. The salaries above are averages from museums with annual budgets of $800K to $2.6 million.

NEMA New England Museum Association, *2004/2005 Salary & Benefits Survey*

SEMC Southeastern Museums Conference, *Southeastern Museums Compensation and Benefits Survey, 2006*
Note: Because SEMC's survey results are organized by budget size and discipline, an overall average salary per position is not available. The salaries above are median figures from history museums with annual budgets of $1 to $3 million.

VAM Virginia Association of Museums, *2005 Salary Survey*

APPENDIX TWO

SALARIES FOR TEN COMMON POSITIONS
AS SURVEYED BY MUSEUM PROFESSIONAL ASSOCIATIONS

These ten jobs were chosen to represent senior-, middle-, and entry-level positions common to different sizes of museums. These salaries were garnered from surveys by museum professional associations with members from throughout the United States. See below for information on the associations.

SURVEY YEAR	AAMD 2007	ACM 2006
DIRECTOR (OVERALL AVERAGE)	216,347	59,500
DIRECTOR (SMALL MUSEUM, FY$/SALARY)	1 to 2.5 mil/70,502	<250K/30,000
DEVELOPMENT OFFICER	107,907	55,000
DEVELOPMENT/ MEMBERSHIP ASSISTANT	41,920	29,000
PUBLIC RELATIONS MANAGER	54,646	34,762
CHIEF CURATOR	90,549	*48,141
CURATORIAL ASSISTANT	32,227	*29,125
REGISTRAR	41,551	n/a
EDUCATION DIRECTOR	67,052	42,801
EDUCATION ASSISTANT	29,960	27,000

AAMD Association of Art Museum Directors, *2007 Salary Survey*
  Note: Membership to AAMD is limited to directors of museums with budgets at or above $2,000,000. Salaries for upper-level positions at these museums will be higher compared to associations that include museums with smaller budgets.

ACM Association of Children's Museums, *Compensation and Benefits Survey 2006*
  Note: ACM's salary figures are median amounts, not the averages of surveyed institutions.

* Because many children's museums have large exhibitions staff and few curators, these salaries reflect the positions of exhibitions director and exhibitions assistant.

APGA 2006	ASTC 2001
103,210	122,444
<250K/51,682	****49,850
74,321	73,787
38,768	n/a
55,458	62,607
**59,043	47,835
n/a	n/a
***45,657	n/a
55,124	67,666
39,581	n/a

APGA American Public Gardens Association, *2006 Compensation and Benefits Study*

** salary is for director of horticulture
*** salary is for collections manager

ASTC Association of Science-Technology Centers, *Science Center Workforce 2001: An ASTC Report*

**** no budget size stated

APPENDIX THREE

ORGANIZATIONS AND WEBSITES
FOR STUDENTS AND MUSEUM PROFESSIONALS

The following organizations and websites either serve the museum community directly or correspond to museum functions as they relate to employment. Sites with employment listings have an asterisk *. Organizations with "AAM SPC" next to them are Standing Professional Committees of the American Association of Museums.

NOTE: website addresses are accurate to the time of this writing only. Should you find a website no longer exists, search for the organization name via web search engines.

THE ACADEMY OF CERTIFIED ARCHIVISTS
www.certifiedarchivists.org

AMERICAN ASSOCIATION FOR MUSEUM VOLUNTEERS
www.ansp.org/hosted/aamv

***AMERICAN ASSOCIATION FOR STATE AND LOCAL HISTORY**
www.aaslh.org

***AMERICAN ASSOCIATION OF MUSEUMS**
www.aam-us.org

***AMERICAN INSTITUTE FOR CONSERVATION
OF HISTORIC & ARTISTIC WORKS**
http://aic.stanford.edu

***AMERICAN LIBRARY ASSOCIATION**
www.ala.org

***AMERICAN MARKETING ASSOCIATION**
www.marketingpower.com

***AMERICAN PUBLIC GARDENS ASSOCIATION**
www.publicgardens.org

ARCHIVES AND INFORMATICS ASSOCIATION
www.archimuse.com

***ART LIBRARIES SOCIETY OF NORTH AMERICA**
www.arlisna.org

***ASSOCIATION FOR LIVING HISTORICAL FARMS
AND AGRICULTURAL MUSEUMS**
www.alhfam.org

*ASSOCIATION OF ART MUSEUM CURATORS
www.artcurators.org

*ASSOCIATION OF ART MUSEUM DIRECTORS
www.aamd.org

ASSOCIATION OF ARTS ADMINISTRATION EDUCATORS
www.artsadministration.org

*ASSOCIATION OF CHILDREN'S MUSEUMS
www.childrensmuseums.org

**ASSOCIATION OF COLLEGE AND
UNIVERSITY MUSEUMS AND GALLERIES**
www.acumg.org

*ASSOCIATION OF FUNDRAISING PROFESSIONALS
www.nsfre.org

*ASSOCIATION OF MIDWEST MUSEUMS
www.midwestmuseums.org

***ASSOCIATION OF SCIENCE
AND TECHNOLOGY CENTERS**
www.astc.org

ASSOCIATION OF SCIENCE MUSEUM DIRECTORS
www.asmd.org

*ASSOCIATION OF ZOOS AND AQUARIUMS
www.aza.org

**BANK STREET COLLEGE LEADERSHIP
IN MUSEUM EDUCATION**
www.bankstreet.edu/gs/leadershipinmuseumed.html

BOARDSOURCE
www.boardsource.org

*CALIFORNIA ASSOCIATION OF MUSEUMS
www.calmuseums.org

**CAMPBELL CENTER
FOR HISTORIC PRESERVATION**
www.campbellcenter.org

*CANADIAN HERITAGE INFORMATION NETWORK
www.chin.gc.ca

*CANADIAN MUSEUMS ASSOCIATION
www.museums.ca

CENTER FOR CURATORIAL LEADERSHIP
www.curatorialleadership.org

*CHRONICLE OF HIGHER EDUCATION
http://chronicle.com

*CHRONICLE OF PHILANTHROPY
www.philanthropy.com

*COLLEGE ART ASSOCIATION
www.collegeart.org

CONSERVATION ONLINE
http://palimpsest.stanford.edu

COUNCIL OF STATE ARCHIVISTS
www.statearchivists.org

CURATORS' COMMITTEE (AAM SPC)
www.curcom.org

**COMMITTEE ON AUDIENCE RESEARCH
AND EVALUATION (AAM SPC)**
www.care-aam.org

EDUCATION COMMITTEE (AAM SPC)
www.edcom.org

FLORIDA ASSOCIATION OF MUSEUMS
www.flamuseums.org

GETTY CONSERVATION INSTITUTE
www.getty.edu/conservation

GETTY LEADERSHIP INSTITUTE
www.getty.edu/leadership

*GLOBAL MUSEUM
www.globalmuseum.org

GUIDESTAR.ORG

HERITAGE PRESERVATION
www.heritagepreservation.org

*HIGHEREDJOBS.COM

*IDEALIST.ORG

INDUSTRIAL DESIGNERS SOCIETY OF AMERICA
www.idsa.org

*INSTITUTE OF CERTIFIED RECORDS MANAGERS
www.icrm.org

INSTITUTE OF MUSEUM AND LIBRARY SERVICES
www.imls.gov

***INTERNATIONAL ASSOCIATION OF
MUSEUM FACILITY ADMINISTRATORS**
www.iamfa.org

**INTERNATIONAL COMMITTEE
ON MUSEUM SECURITY**
user.chollian.net/~pll/public_html/icms

INTERNATIONAL COUNCIL OF MUSEUMS (ICOM)
http://icom.museum

INTERNATIONAL PLANETARIUM SOCIETY
www.ips-planetarium.org

*JOURNALISMJOBS.COM

*MEDIABISTRO.COM

MEDIA AND TECHNOLOGY COMMITTEE (AAM SPC)
www.mediaandtechnology.org

*MID-ATLANTIC ASSOCIATION OF MUSEUMS
www.midatlanticmuseums.org

*MOUNTAIN-PLAINS MUSEUMS ASSOCIATION
www.mpma.net

MUSEUM ASSOCIATION OF NEW YORK
www.manyonline.org

*MUSEUM COMPUTER NETWORK
www.mcn.edu
(see their list-serve for job postings)

MUSEUM EDUCATION ROUNDTABLE
www.mer-online.org

MUSEUM-ED
www.museum-ed.org

***MUSEUM EMPLOYMENT RESOURCE CENTER**
www.museum-employment.com

***MUSEUMJOBS.COM**

***MUSEUM-L** [listserve for museum professionals]
http://home.ease.lsoft.com/scripts/wa.exe?A0=museum-l

***MUSEUMMARKET.COM**

***MUSEUM STORE ASSOCIATION**
www.museumdistrict.com

MUSEUM STUFF
www.museumstuff.com

MUSEUM TRUSTEE ASSOCIATION
www.mta-hq.org

MUSEUMSUSA.ORG

NATIONAL ART EDUCATION ASSOCIATION
www.naea-reston.org

***NATIONAL ASSOCIATION
FOR MUSEUM EXHIBITION (AAM SPC)**
www.n-a-m-e.org

***NATIONAL ASSOCIATION OF
GOVERNMENT ARCHIVES AND RECORDS
ADMINISTRATORS**
www.nagara.org

**NATIONAL CENTER FOR PRESERVATION
TECHNOLOGY AND TRAINING**
www.ncptt.nps.gov

***NATIONAL COUNCIL ON PUBLIC HISTORY**
www.ncph.org

NATIONAL DOCENT SYMPOSIUM COUNCIL
www.docents.net

*NATIONAL TRUST FOR HISTORIC PRESERVATION
www.nationaltrust.org

NATURAL SCIENCE COLLECTIONS ALLIANCE
www.nscalliance.org

*NEW ENGLAND MUSEUM ASSOCIATION
www.nemanet.org

*NONPROFIT.CAREERBUILDER.COM

*NONPROFITCAREERS.COM

*NONPROFITOYSTER.COM

***PACKING, ARTHANDLING & CRATING
INFORMATION NETWORK (AAM SPC)**
www.pacin.org

PR AND MARKETING COMMITTEE (AAM SPC)
www.pram-aam.org

PRESERVATION DIRECTORY.COM
www.preservationdirectory.com

*PRWEEKJOBS.COM

*PUBLIC HISTORY RESOURCE CENTER
www.publichistory.org

*PUBLIC RELATIONS SOCIETY OF AMERICA
http://prsa.com

*PUBLISHERSMARKETPLACE.COM

*REGISTRARS COMMITTEE (AAM SPC)
www.rcaam.org

*SCIENCEJOBS.COM

*SECURITYJOBS.NET

*SMALL MUSEUM ASSOCIATION
www.smallmuseum.org

**SMITHSONIAN INSTITUTION CENTER FOR
EDUCATION AND MUSEUM STUDIES**
http://museumstudies.si.edu

**SMITHSONIAN INSTITUTION
RESEARCH INFORMATION SYSTEM**
www.siris.si.edu

*SOCIETY FOR AMERICAN ARCHEOLOGY
www.saa.org
***SOCIETY FOR ENVIRONMENTAL
GRAPHIC DESIGN**
www.segd.org

***SOCIETY FOR HUMAN
RESOURCE MANAGEMENT**
www.shrm.org

*SOCIETY OF AMERICAN ARCHIVISTS
www.archivists.org

*SOUTHEASTERN MUSEUMS CONFERENCE
www.semcdirect.net

*SPECIAL LIBRARIES ASSOCIATION
www.sla.org

TECHSOUP.ORG

*TEXAS ASSOCIATION OF MUSEUMS
www.io.com/~tam

***UNIVERSITY OF LEICESTER,
DEPARTMENT OF MUSEUM STUDIES**
www.le.ac.uk/ms

VIRGINIA ASSOCIATION OF MUSEUMS
www.vamuseums.org

*VISUAL RESOURCES ASSOCIATION
www.vraweb.org

*WESTERN MUSEUMS ASSOCIATION
www.westmuse.org

*WORKINPR.COM

SELECTED BIBLIOGRAPHY

NOTE: for published salary surveys, see Appendixes One and Two.

Anderson, Gail, ed. *Reinventing the Museum, Historical and Contemporary Perspectives on the Paradigm Shift.* Lanham, Maryland: AltaMira Press, 2004.

Bates, G. W., ed. *Museum Jobs from A–Z. What They Are, How to Prepare, and Where to Find Them,* rev. ed. Ft. Lauderdale, Florida: Bantax Museum Publishing, 1994.

Bryck, Nancy Villa. "Reports of Our Death Have Been Greatly Exaggerated: Reconsidering the Curator." *Museum News.* Vol. 80, No. 2, pp. 39–41, 67, 69, 71, March/April 2001.

Bunch, Lonnie. "Flies in the Buttermilk: Museums, Diversity, and the Will to Change." *Museum News.* Vol. 79, No. 4, pp. 32–36, July/August, 2000.

Burcaw, G. Ellis. *Introduction to Museum Work,* 3rd ed. Walnut Creek, California: AltaMira Press, published in cooperation with the American Association for State and Local History, 1997.

Carbonell, Bettina Messias, ed. *Museum Studies: An Anthology of Contexts.* Oxford, England: Blackwell Publishers, 2003.

Camenson, Blythe. *Opportunities in Museum Careers.* Lincolnwood, Illinois: VGM Career Horizons, 1996.

Chambers, Elizabeth A. "The Troublesome Matter of the Changing Role of the Curator." Awarded paper from the Museum Studies Program, George Washington University, Washington, DC, 2001, available online at: http://www.gwu.edu/~mstd/publications.htm (accessed August 11, 2005).

Chen, Yi-Chien. "Educating Art Museum Professionals: The Current State of Museum Studies Programs in the United States." Dissertation, Department of Art Education, Florida State University, Tallahassee, 2004.
Available online at: http://etd.lib.fsu.edu/theses/available/etd-07132004-121102 (accessed October 5, 2005).

Danilov, Victor J. *Museum Careers and Training: A Professional Guide.* Westport, Connecticut: Greenwood Press, 1994.

Dubberly, Sara, ed. *Careers in Museum: A Variety of Vocations.* Professional Practices Series. Washington, DC: American Association of Museums, 1992.

Genoways, Hugh H. and Lynne M. Ireland. *Museum Administration: An Introduction.* Walnut Creek, California: AltaMira Press, 2003.

Glaser, Jane R. and Artemis A. Zenotou. *Museums: A Place to Work, Planning Museum Careers.* New York: Routledge, 1996.

Marty, Paul F. "So You Want to Work in a Museum: Guiding the Careers of Future Museum Information Specialists." *Journal for Library and Information Science.* Vol. 46, no. 2, pp. 115–133, Spring, 2005.

Marty, Paul F., W. Boyd Rayward, and Michael B. Twidale. "Museum Informatics." *Annual Review of Information Science and Technology.* Vol. 37, pp. 259–294, 2003.

Merritt, Elizabeth E., ed. *2003 Museum Financial Information.* Washington, DC: American Association of Museums, 2003.

Merritt, Elizabeth E., ed. *2006 Museum Financial Information.* Washington, DC: American Association of Museums, 2006.

Museum Data Collection Report and Analysis. Washington, DC: Institute of Museum and Library Services, 2005. Available online at: http://www.imls.gov/pubs/pdf/Museum_Data_Collection.pdf (accessed August 10, 2005).

Preston, Jane. *Museums in the United States at the Turn of the Millennium: An Industry Note.* Cambridge, Massachusetts: John F. Kennedy School of Government, Harvard University Press, 2001.

Schwarzer, Marjorie. "Are Directors Burning Out?" *Museum News.* Vol. 81, No. 3, pp. 43–49, 67, May/June 2002.

Schwarzer, Marjorie. *Graduate Training in Museum Studies: What Students Need to Know.* Washington, DC: American Association of Museums, 2001.

Schwarzer, Marjorie. *Riches, Rivals, and Radicals: 100 Years of Museums in America.* Washington, DC: American Association of Museums, 2006.

Spiess II, Philip D. "Museum Studies: Are They Doing Their Job?" *Museum News.* Vol. 75, No. 6, pp. 32–43, 67, November/December, 1996.

Sterling, Bruce. "The Wonderful World of Storytelling." Speech delivered at the Computer Game Developers Conference, San Jose, CA, 1991.

Twombly, Eric C. "Executive Compensation in the Nonprofit Sector; A Focus on Arts and Cultural Organizations." Washington, DC: Urban Institute, 2002.

Washburn, Wilcomb E. "Education and the New Elite: American Museums in the 1980s and 1990s." *Museum News.* Vol. 75, No. 2, pp. 60–65, March/April, 1996.

Weil, Stephen. "From Being *about* Something to Being *for* Someone." *Daedalus: The Journal of the American Academy of Arts and Sciences.* Vol. 128, No. 3, pp. 229–258, summer 1999.

INDEX

ABOUT THE AUTHOR

N. Elizabeth Schlatter is deputy director and curator of exhibitions of the University of Richmond Museums, Richmond, Virginia, where she has worked since 2000. Her career includes administrative and programmatic positions at the Smithsonian Institution, Washington, DC, and the Contemporary Arts Museum, Houston, Texas. With an M.A. in Art History from George Washington University, she has curated numerous exhibitions of modern and contemporary art; published articles, reviews, and catalog essays; and presented papers on related topics at regional and national conferences. She is author of the ebook *Become an Art Curator*.